A Cat's Lesson
Mr Perkins goes to school

First Published in the UK 2025

Copyright © 2025 by Suzanne Stephenson

All rights reserved. No part of this publication may be reproduced or transmitted, in any form or by any means, without permission of the publishers or author. Excepting brief quotes used in reviews.

Any reference to real names and places are purely fictional and are constructs of the author. Any offence the references produce is unintentional and in no way reflects the reality of any locations or people involved.

ISBN: 978-1-917411-31-8

A Cat's Lesson

Mr Perkins goes to school

Written and illustrated by

Suzanne Stephenson

Also by the author

Bearswood End
Mr Perkins Takes Charge
A Cat's Judgement
The World According To Patrick White
Santa Pig, The Trials of Patrick White
The Tale of Philida Thrush

'Forever Waste'
A light romantic novel & legal satire

Beginnings

(i)

The kennel door slammed shut and Winnie the retriever-setter cross looked dismally out through the bars of what seemed to be a canine prison but was in reality her rescue haven until someone could find her a new home. Bewildered and scared she had no way of knowing that her loving owner had died suddenly in the supermarket car park of heart failure and her owner's family had long since emigrated to Australia. She did not know that her owner's nephew had transferred a large donation to the dog rescue kennels to assist with her care until she had a new home. She did not know the long wait she had spent alone, locked in the house was not her owner's fault.

She had been in this place once before and had a dim memory of it. She looked at the kennel maid through the bars and her eyes said 'betrayed' at the closing door and her front paws shook slightly. She had been here weeks, but things didn't seem to get better.

The kennel maid kneeled down and said in soft tones,

"It will be alright you know… you are beautiful… someone will soon come and adopt you."

She continued talking in soft tones to the frightened dog for about twenty minutes and then she said,

"Right, I will be back later to give you a walk," and with that she walked away.

After a short time had elapsed a small black shadow appeared on a wall followed by a small black form. The cat went up to the bars of the door and rubbed noses with the unhappy dog. He sat down and purred. The dog seemed to find the purring soothing and lay down. Gradually the dog seemed to drift off to sleep. When the kennel maid returned after a couple of hours the cat was nowhere to be seen.

"You seem calmer now," she said as she opened the door and attached a leash to the dog. "Shall we have a nice little walk now?" Winnie wagged her tail.

(ii)

At the same time as the kennel door slammed shut, so did the back of the remover's van. Lenny (short for Leonora) looked disconsolately into the hallway of her new home and sat down heavily on the doorstep and burst into tears. She had never wanted to move house, to move away from her friends and her school. But she had no say in the matter. Mum said that she should not be so selfish.

"Lenny," said Mum, "your dad has commuted a round trip of nearly four hours every working day in the office for over two years and now he is to be an equity partner it will not do for him to take so many days working from home. You do not want to get in the way of his career."

Lenny had not replied because she knew it would do no good, but Mum persisted,

"You will make new friends... After all, I will have to make adjustments as well since I am moving job too..." Lenny said nothing, but Mum had added, "And maybe we will get a dog."

As Lenny sat crying, she wondered whether her mother had meant it. Her father was a tall, larger than life man so there was no telling what he would think. He had mentioned having a dog as a boy, it was true, and Granny and Grandad had a pair of Scottie dogs. Mum had grown up with cats and Nanny and Gramps had a fine pair of tortoiseshell cats. It was a pity that the new house was not much closer to her grandparents than her previous home. She found a tissue in her sleeve and blew her nose.

A small black form appeared, and she felt something rub against her legs. It was a black cat with glowing yellow eyes. Somehow, she felt as if she knew him, and he knew her. She stroked him and he purred loudly.

"Do you live around here, purry puss?" she asked. He looked inscrutable.

She stroked him for quite some time and the purring made her feel better.

She got up and ran into the house. "Mum," she called, "there is a lovely black cat."

"What... what?" said her mother from somewhere in the interior of the house. They both headed to the front door. The cat was nowhere to be seen.

"Never mind," said Mum, "he was probably some stray... But we will definitely get a dog like I promised you."

Lenny felt reassured by her mother's comment.

Chapter 1

Leonora

Lenny had been thrilled by her tenth birthday party. All her friends from school had come. The weather was fine so most of the time was spent outside including the magic show from the entertainers hired by her parents. How Lenny loved the garden which went down to a little wood, where there was a swing attached to an old chestnut tree. She loved the rose garden with its little path where she would play skipping and other games. She loved the grassy area currently enjoyed by her friends.

She loved the summerhouse which was big enough to accommodate the buffet her mum had laid out with the centrepiece being a two tiered pink cake. She loved that she had at least another whole year ahead of her at her primary school with her best friends. It was only May. She knew that her best friends and herself had a reasonable chance of going to the same high school, so everything seemed good.

She had loved the pink party dress Mum had got her. It had been great to see it hung up in her room. She loved the view out to the garden from her room. When most of her friends had gone home, she and her two best friends Janey and Rosie had gone to her room and tried on some of her new birthday clothes and talked about the forthcoming school outing to the wildlife park.

She was sure her parents Tony and Kate were chatting with Janey and Rosie's parents about future play dates. Tony was a tall affable man. Being above average height with chestnut curls and a loud laugh he reminded her of a good-tempered bear. Work kept him very busy, so she did not see so much of him in the week as his office where he practiced commercial law was some distance from home. At the weekend when he wasn't out running, he tried to spend time with her. Kate her mother was more available. Kate worked in something called 'Listing' at the local court. Lenny had originally wondered why her mother made lists of things at the court but had recently learned that Kate was actually putting cases in diaries for hearing. Life was good; fleetingly she would sometimes wish she was a little closer to her grandparents and wish she had a cat or a dog.

After everyone had gone home Tony and Kate Tadworth had become serious and had asked her to sit down in the living room. Kate said,

"Lenny, darling, Daddy is becoming an equity partner of Rinewater Standing."

Lenny had understood from hearing the grownups talk that it was a good thing for her father to become an equity partner in the law firm where he worked so she said,

"Well done, Daddy."

Tony cleared his throat. "I will need to be on hand more at the firm. I will not be able to be an equity partner by working from home and with a long commute. I did think about taking a flat or room for weekdays, but I felt we would not be having a proper family life so we will be moving house."

Lenny looked stunned and stammered,

"What about Mum's job? Will I be able to continue at my school?"

Kate answered, "I have accepted a new job as a paralegal at Rinewater Standing in their family litigation department… and we have identified a nice new school for you, as you would be too far from your current school."

Lenny would have normally asked what a paralegal did and in other circumstances would have been pleased to hear of her mother assisting on legal cases at the law firm. But the thought of changing schools as well as moving house was hitting her like a bombshell. She felt shivers down her spine. Tears started to well up.

"But what about my friends? What about my last year at primary school?" she asked.

Mum responded,

"I am sure you will make new friends, and you would have changed school anyway in another year."

Lenny was sobbing. "What about my room and our lovely garden?"

"Now, now," said Dad, "you will have a super new room and a great garden to play in. We have been very lucky to get a cash buyer for this house, and Mum and I have found a great place for our new home."

So that was what Mum and Dad had been doing while she had a couple of weekends with each set of grandparents - plotting this move. She presumed they realised she would not be happy about it, so they had arranged things behind her back. A little later she went and spoke to Midge and Mabel her guinea pigs. Stroking them on her lap seemed reassuring but it did not get over the fact she did not want to move.

During the last few weeks of term her schoolwork marks seemed to slip. She spent a lot of time hunched up on a bench in a corner at breaktime.

"Come on, Lenny," said Janey, "come and join in with us and our game." Lenny tried to muster some enthusiasm.

One weekend at the very beginning of July she found herself whisked away on Sunday morning.

"We are staying in a hotel for one night," said Mum as Dad raced up the motorway, "so we should be able to show you the new house and the village this afternoon and you can see the new school on Monday morning before we go home. Oh, and you may remember old Aunt Lavinia. She lives nearby so we will call in on her for a cup of tea as well."

Lenny did remember Aunt Lavinia, but she wished the memories had been more pleasant. She knew Aunt Lavinia was Granny's cousin. Her earliest memory of her dated from before she was three years old, so it was somewhat vague. Aunt Lavinia had seemed very tall to her at that time. With her hair in a grey bun and wire rimmed glasses and a longish black and purple dress, Aunt Lavinia's angular frame reminded Lenny of a witch in a story book. She had bent down and pinched Lenny's cheek and said,

"You are very small, my child."

At that time Aunt Lavinia had a little Scottie dog called Dickie, and Lenny and Dickie had enjoyed a game of chase running up and down and round the furniture and everyone's legs. Lenny recalled this made Aunt Lavinia somewhat annoyed. Sadly, Lenny understood Dickie was not around anymore. She had seen Aunt Lavinia a couple of times since at family parties and her parents continued to exchange news with her. Aunt Lavinia looked very serious and fierce each time she saw her. She recalled Aunt Lavinia had been a teacher, and it seemed she still appeared to like to tell people what to do; once she could recall Aunt Lavinia holding forth loudly about art and telling the whole family her favourite artistic subject was still lives of vegetables. The last contact with Aunt Lavinia had been prior to last Christmas, just before her school's Christmas fair.

In the post there been an envelope addressed to Miss Leonora Tadworth. It was unusual for her to receive her own post. Inside the envelope was a Christmas card with a Nativity scene. She opened the card, and a crisp ten pound note fell out. Leonora was thrilled with this receipt but then she read the words inside the card.

'My dear little Leonora,

I hear you are having a school Christmas fair for charity. I enclose a £10 note so the charity can benefit by you buying something at the Christmas fair to send to me.

With seasonal greetings,

Aunt Lavinia.'

Lenny had passed the card and the money to her mother without saying anything and had run up to her room.

As Lenny sat in the car a rain shower left droplets on the window and a tear rolled down her cheek. She breathed in heavily and fought back her tears. Her father took an exit from the motorway, but they did not proceed into the city to her father's office. After a couple of miles, they turned off the main road onto a country lane. There was a finger-board sign saying 'Willowrose by Stow 5 ½ miles, Twelve Tree Bottom 7 miles'. Next to it was a large twisted old oak tree with some branches almost touching the ground. There were pleasing vistas of fields, hedges and rolling hills each side of the road. Soon there was a sign which read 'Welcome to Willowrose by Stow'.

First, they passed a bland new housing development. Lenny hoped they were not living there. Then they were soon in the village centre where she could see some pretty cottages, a village shop, an antique shop, a Chinese takeaway and a pub. They slowed down but did not stop.

"Look, there is the school," said Mum. There was a hotch-potch of buildings including a Victorian Schoolhouse, a mid-twentieth century hall and some portacabins and there appeared to be a large field behind the buildings, with a track to one side with a wobbly sign saying, 'Rose Bungalows 1-4'. On the metal playground fence in front of the school was a sign which read 'Willowrose Primary Academy School, Headteacher Adrianne Deamer'. Next to the school there was an ancient church with an extensive churchyard surrounded by yews and willows with a small sign by an arched gateway which read 'St Rita's Church, *Reverend Marchbanks'*.

They drove out of the village centre past a playground and a duckpond. They slowed a little as they passed a tarmac car park and a barn-type building with a large sign which read 'The Impossible Pig, Farm shop'. Lenny thought it an odd name but was soon distracted by the car slowing and coming to a halt further up the lane.

They came to a halt outside a property with tall unkempt hedges and an estate agent's board poking wonkily out of the foliage with bold letters 'Sold' on it. There was a wide gateway with five-bar gates one of which was slightly open. There was a dilapidated sign on the gate reading 'Woodland View'. The house was mainly built of mellow stone but visible from the road was a porch built of conservatory material and a red brick extension to the ground floor at one side which was rather jarringly dissimilar to the main house. There was a separate red brick construction to one side which appeared to be a pair of garages and there was also a large gravel driveway area which led to the house and garages. The front garden was an overgrown tangled mess. Lenny thought she saw a cat disappear into the undergrowth.

Mum said, "I am afraid we can't go inside because we don't have a key yet, but I am sure no-one would mind if we walked around the garden today since the house is empty."

Lenny said nothing but followed her parents out of the car. They walked around to the back of the house where she could see a conservatory ran along the entire back of the original house opening onto a patio area made of old mellow stone. There was a slightly ramshackle rear enclosed porch on the brick extension. There was also a stone well with a roof on it in the middle of the patio with a weathervane in the shape of a cat on top of its roof. A lawn which needed cutting ran down a gentle slope away from the patio and led to a wicker arch with plants cascading over it. She could make out an orchard area just beyond the archway. To one side of the archway was a stone bird bath and a stone statue of a cat enigmatically looking at the bird bath. There appeared to be another old house with extensive gardens to one side of the property and open fields to the other side of the property. There was a small wood on the other side of the road.

"It has so much potential," said Dad, "and it will be great for entertaining the partners, once tidied up."

"What about the summerhouse?" stammered Lenny.

"Well, that will stay behind," said Dad. "We will see if we need one as there is a huge conservatory."

"And my swing?" she queried.

"You are getting a bit big for swings," answered her father. Lenny choked back her tears.

They went back to the front of the house and Mum pointed to a window of what seemed to be an attic room.

"Your room will be up there," said Mum. "It's a very big space, much bigger than your present room. You will have views of the wood."

As they turned to return to the car, Lenny thought she saw a small pair of yellow eyes looking at her from out of the undergrowth of the little wood. She said nothing. Dad turned the car round and within a couple of minutes they were parked in front of a picturesque cottage in the village centre.

"Hello, Auntie," said Dad to Aunt Lavinia as she opened the door.

"Come inside, my dears, I have tea on the table for you," replied Aunt Lavinia.

Lenny made use of the facilities before she took her place at the dining room table. Aunt Lavinia's downstairs cloakroom was white and spotless and very plain except for a large photograph in a gold frame. It was a picture of Dickie.

Aunt Lavinia had placed a tray with a pot of tea in a bone china teapot together with a jug of hot water and a jug of milk on the lace tablecloth near a tray of teacups and a sugar basin. There were four places set with matching china plates and cake forks and teaspoons and little white linen napkins. The pattern on the china was of Scottie dogs. Also on the table was a large plate of tiny sandwiches and a large cake with white icing which appeared to have partly run off the cake.

"Very traditional," said Dad. Lenny thought it looked very old-fashioned. She was offered a sandwich and politely took one. Then she bit into it. The bread was somewhat dry, and the filling consisted of mashed hardboiled egg, cress and some crushed eggshell. She tried not to retch and gulped it down.

"You do seem hungry, my dear," said Auntie Lavinia looking at her empty plate.

Lenny found she had no option but to take another sandwich. After several minutes of nibbling round the edges she took courage and bit into the filling. This sandwich appeared to contain some type of mashed tinned fish together with egg… something was again ominously crunchy.

Lenny did not finish her sandwich but looked sweetly at Aunt Lavinia.

"Great Auntie, if I finish this sandwich, I won't have room for your lovely looking cake."

Aunt Lavinia beamed and said, "Of course you must try the cake. I made it myself."

Albeit the cake looked strange, it actually was an unexciting but pleasant lemon sponge.

As they left, Aunt Lavinia said wistfully, "When you have moved, please do visit often. I don't see as many people as when I used to walk Dickie. With my bad legs I couldn't do long walks."

As they drove to the hotel Lenny asked why Aunt Lavinia had not got another pet. Mum responded, "I think she is set in her ways and cannot picture a situation where she has a different pet."

They spent the night at a chain hotel with burger place next door, adjacent to the motorway junction. Next morning they returned to the village and Mum and Dad took her into the school. The children were in class so the playground was empty but there was a background hum of children's voices. Miss Deamer met them at the doorway, introducing herself, and then took them swiftly to her office where there was another woman sat in the corner. Leonora could see that Miss Deamer was a little older than her parents. She had neatly styled black hair and wore a dark blue trouser suit. The woman in the corner was somewhat older and had a shock of unruly red and grey curly hair.

Miss Deamer introduced her. "This is Miss Dymock, my deputy who is also in charge of all our music at the school and is our main Year 6 teacher."

Miss Dymock said nothing and just nodded at Leonora and her parents.

Miss Deamer said, "I understand from the information given by yourselves and Leonora's old school that Leonora was doing well in most subject areas until recently but has slipped back a little. I hope we can reassure you that we are up to tackling most issues here."

A conversation followed between Mum and Dad and Miss Deamer. Lenny didn't really listen to much of it until Miss Deamer said,

"This school used to be called after St Rita, like the church. St Rita is the Patron Saint of the Impossible. When the school became an Academy there was overwhelming support to change its name from 'St Rita of the

Impossible Primary School'. You can imagine even though the school did well in league tables, the name was unhelpful in many respects. The name has been kept for one or two limited purposes, for example the parent-teacher football team call themselves 'the Impossibles'."

Lenny thought she might now understand the name of the farm shop and smiled briefly. Miss Dymock suddenly barked at her,

"Do you play an instrument or sing?"

"N… no Miss," replied Lenny.

"Shame," said Miss Dymock sourly. "We will have to teach you."

The interview finished with Miss Deamer and Miss Dymock taking the family on a brief tour of the school. They did not enter the classrooms as lessons were in session. Lenny could see the school had the same types of facilities as her old school but dotted about in different buildings. Miss Deamer walked swiftly while Miss Dymock seemed to hobble at the rear. She was clad in a strange long knitted garment and somehow, she reminded Lenny of a large sheep.

The tour finished at the main gates of the school.

"We look forward to Leonora joining us for Year 6 in the near future, hopefully in September," said Miss Deamer. Miss Dymock scowled. Lenny was not sure if she looked forward to joining the school.

As she got in the car Lenny thought she saw a black cat fleetingly pass the school entrance. It looked a bit like the weathervane on the old well and it gave her an unexpected thought that maybe it would bring her luck. Soon she dismissed the idea from her thoughts.

Chapter 2

Winnie

Winnie sat in her kennel and wished she had a person of her very own… or better still more than one. She used to have people and animal friends and companions. She had been in the kennel for a few months now. It was not the first time she had been there.

Her earliest memory was of cuddling up to her mother and her brothers and sisters. She recalled feeling warm and cosy and as she got bigger playing chase with her siblings and tossing squeaky toys in the air and pulling on some ropy things when a man and woman came. She now knew that's what they were; at the time she thought they were just a bit big and scary. Once she was put in a basket with her siblings and taken in a car to a person called a 'vet'. It was a bit frightening, and she didn't like being poked about but at least she shared this experience with her brothers and sisters.

The man and the woman talked to the puppies now and then. The man would say to the woman, "Don't get too fond of them, they will have to go to new homes as soon as we can sell them. Breeding these puppies is for money, not for fun."

Sometimes the woman would sigh and say, "Funny old business, isn't it."

One day the man leant down and picked her up roughly.

"Hey, puppy, reckon I got a new home for you."

She was carried outside away from her mother. The man spoke to another man.

"Look how she wriggles around... see. What do you think? Could she join your pack?"

"I dunno," said the second man who looked big and strong and swarthy. "I had been thinking more about a hound or even a Rotty to chase them hares... but she looks a strong little thing. I'll give 'er a go."

Before long Winnie was shoved in a box and placed in a car. She sat in near darkness as they journeyed for less than an hour. She was carried to a place where there was yapping and howling from other dogs. The man lifted her out of the box. A youngish woman said, "She's cute. What shall we call her?"

The man replied gruffly, "Call her what you like... but I don't want her to be cute. I want her to be a hunter."

"Okay, okay, Kenny," said the woman, "I'll call her Winnie. You got a Winston so you may as well have a Winnie."

The man snarled at the woman, "Look, Sabrina, this ain't some soft petting farm... I've told you that. These are working dogs."

Winston, who Winnie later discovered was something called a Pitbull, growled from behind some bars. Winnie found herself pushed into a kennel with two other young dogs, an emaciated young boxer dog and a tiny shivering Jack Russell puppy. There was no bedding, no heating... just a bit of straw at the back of the kennel. The floor was dirty and there was no food. The man and woman left. Winnie sat there and howled.

After what seemed an age, the man returned and threw a piece of unpleasant looking raw meat into the kennel.

"Go on," he said, "let's see if any of you have any fight in you."

The boxer dog withdrew into a corner. Winnie was hungry so she attempted to tear some pieces of meat away from the hunk and golloped them down. The little Jack Russell was attempting to lick the hunk of meat.

The unpleasant man peered at the boxer dog. "Useless... you won't last... They can eat you if you won't fight."

When the man had gone Winnie bit off some more pieces of meat. First, she put a chunk down in front of the Jack Russell who gobbled down the piece and then she put a piece down in front of the boxer. She licked his face as her mother had done to her and tentatively, he began to eat the piece of meat. She went back to the hunk of meat and took another piece for herself but then bit off more pieces for her new friends until it was all gone. This was the pattern for several days. Sometimes the man would take Winston and a couple of the fiercer dogs out at night. Sometimes the woman Sabrina would creep in and gently open the kennel door to Winnie and her companions and throw something into the enclosure, be it bread crusts or broken biscuits and say,

"Shhh. He doesn't need to know."

Sabrina was painfully thin and quite dishevelled herself. She was often as cowed as the skinny boxer and the little Jack Russell.

"I'll soon take that Winnie dog and the useless other two out on the hunt," said the man one night.

"Please," said Sabrina, "I don't think they're ready." Her voice had a tearful pleading tone.

The man cuffed her around the face. "They are ready when I say they are ready... no arguments. I put bread on the table, so you do as I say. You shouldn't have married me if you didn't like the lifestyle."

Winnie didn't understand what was meant but she was learning to understand that Sabrina was as much a prisoner as she was. While the man went out that night Sabrina made some effort to tidy the kennels. She went to look for some newspapers and sat on an old bucket outside, old duffel coat pulled around her, trying to sort out the heap of papers. A little voice said,

"Miaow," and a black cat with yellow eyes looked up at her.

"Where did you come from?" asked Sabrina and the cat purred as she stroked him. Then he scrabbled in the papers with his two front paws.

"Hey, please, I need them," said Sabrina pulling the papers from under his paws.

A headline struck her immediately. It read 'Police seek Hare Coursing

Gang'. She read the article which mentioned not only the cruelty to the hares and dogs involved but the criminal damage to fences, crops and even farm buildings. It highlighted the criminal nature of the gangs and asked the public to give information, anonymous if need be. A shiver went down Sabrina's back.

She tried to straighten out the rest of the papers and a leaflet dropped out headed 'Confidential helpline for abuse victims'.

The cat purred and gazed at her with his hypnotic eyes. She spoke to him as if he was a person. "I shouldn't have let him sweep me off my feet… Good thing we haven't got a kid. Worst six months I've had in my life… Says he will kill me if I try to leave…"

Sabrina thought of how different it had been when she had worked part-time at a coffee shop in the city while doing some part-time courses on children's welfare. Her husband, as he was now, had been a customer and had flattered her like no-one else had done. Kenny, as he liked to be called, had taken her to nightclubs, usually with gambling involved. Kenny wasn't his real name; it was a nickname he liked, being the name of a famous criminal, Kenny Noye. He didn't have any connections with that particular criminal but some of his friends and acquaintances seemed either very colourful or quite mysterious.

Life seemed very exciting. It was a world away from living in a flat with her parents and part-time work in a coffee shop. In due course Kenny swept her away on a short break to Las Vegas and while there had sweet talked her to the wedding chapel.

On their return Sabrina called once at her family home to collect some clothes. Her mother had just said, "Marry in haste, repent at leisure," and looked upset. Since then, she had not been home; she had been taken to this isolated location which her husband had previously said was his 'country cottage' but was in reality a ramshackle collection of sheds and an old mobile home. She didn't drive and her mobile phone quickly seemed to disappear. There was no nearby bus route, and they were about two miles from any other habitation. She supposed her parents were busy with the rest of the family and their jobs and had not tried to find her because they assumed she had just gone off with her husband. On the nights Kenny had disappeared hare coursing, dog fighting or doing something even more nefarious Sabrina had never had the courage to run away. She just tried to do her best for the dogs.

The cat purred loudly and looked enigmatic. Sabrina said, "You are a real Mr Purr-kins." Then she stuffed the newspaper article in her coat pocket and read the leaflet from beginning to end. She looked up as she was also putting it in her pocket. The cat was gone.

A few nights later the man took Winston, a savage mutt, out, but also yanked the skinny terrified boxer out of the kennel.

"Time, he earned his keep," he said and when Sabrina said, "Please, no," he aimed a savage kick to her shins as he passed.

He returned in the early hours of the morning without the boxer. Winston had blood on his muzzle and was limping.

"Useless bloody dogs… they turned on that scraggy thing… Had to beat Winston off so I could bring him back," shouted the man who continued to curse and swear.

"Where is the dog?" queried Sabrina about the boxer.

"Dead," was the one word answer.

"Right, I'm off for a shower… You see to Winston and the others," continued the man who then left.

Sabrina knelt down and whispered to Winnie and the Jack Russell, "Right, I have to leave and take my chances now. But I will ring the police and the RSPCA as soon as I can. I cannot let things carry on as they are." A tear rolled down her cheek, "I'm so sorry…"

Her voice tailed off as she made for the door. Then Winnie could initially sense the rhythm of running feet… then quiet.

Winnie and the Jack Russell cowered in their kennel. Winston whimpered with pain. Hours passed. No-one came with any food.

In the early hours of the following morning the man appeared with a bucket of rotting meat. He shouted at the dogs,

"That bitch has done a runner so you need not think I will be soft like her."

Suddenly, there was a tremendous noise of boots, car engines and shouting.

"Police, we have a warrant," shouted a voice of authority.

Soon, Winnie found herself grabbed by gloved hands and placed in a large container in the back of a van. A kindly voice said,

"It's going to be okay, lass."

Winnie could not help shaking. It was not long, however, before she found herself at what the humans called 'The dog rescue kennels'. It still felt like a prison, but her cage was clean. The little Jack Russell was in a nearby kennel. The voices were friendly. She was given plenty to eat. She was taken out from time to time on a lead for what they called 'walkies'. There were several trips in the van to what they called the 'vets'. She had 'jabs', and she was 'spayed' which was rather more uncomfortable. People played with her from time to time and tried to be kind.

One day one of the kindly humans said, "I think you are ready for a proper home, and I want you to be a good girl when I introduce you to someone."

She was aware that not long ago the Jack Russell had left for what they called a 'proper home'.

Winnie was taken out on her lead to a garden area and there sitting on a bench was an older human who was introduced to her as Ron.

He stood up and bent down and started stroking her. "Hello, my lovely, it's so nice to meet you." She wagged her tail cautiously. Ron spoke to the kennel maid.

"What's her name?" he queried, meanwhile producing a dog treat from his pocket which he proffered to the curious dog.

"Well," said the maid, "we are not altogether sure, but we call her Winnie. We did have a tearful enquiry from a lady who wouldn't give her name. She claimed she was the one who reported the dreadful place where this one and the others were found to the RSPCA and the police. From what she said we think this dog is called Winnie. And the name has stuck."

"Are you Winnie?" asked Ron. Winnie wagged her tail. The human seemed to be her sort of person… indeed he appeared to be the human she wanted to have as her very own person.

"Is she house trained?" he queried.

"We have her kennel trained so it shouldn't be too hard to house train her," was the reply.

"I think she is gorgeous. I think she will be a good friend for me," said Ron. "I live on my own so we can be company for each other."

It was only a couple of weeks before Winnie found herself loaded into Ron's little car. She soon arrived at Ron's bungalow and Ron and her became almost inseparable. Every day they could be seen walking on Ron's street, and she would sniff the doggy friends she met and wag her tail. She would lie at his feet when he watched TV. Plentiful bowls of dog food came her way. Occasionally she got a little treat from his plate. She had a dog basket she sometimes used in the day, but she slept on the end of his bed at night. Sometimes she would go to the garden of a place he called the 'pub' and share a sausage with him while Ron drank stuff called beer. Ron's friends would stroke her and call her a 'good girl', and he would play cards with them in that garden. Occasionally people called at Ron's bungalow including a man called 'my nephew Reg' or 'my nephew in the forces'. Ron spoke on the telephone frequently to people he called 'the family in Australia'. Life had a certain rhythm to it and was good. Just now and again Winnie wondered if she would ever meet Sabrina again. She knew she had liked her.

After about two years when Winnie's rescue became a distant memory, it became very hot.

"Phew," Ron would say, looking in pain, "this hot summer is making my chest go all of a flutter."

He would wipe the sweat from his red face with a handkerchief. He would still go off in his little car to do his weekly shop at the local supermarket. Before he left, he would always fill Winnie's water bowl and give her a handful of treats. One day she sat in the hallway waiting for him, but he did not come back. It got dark and she started to howl and scratch at the door. Ron didn't come. After a while she heard a gentle miaowing and purring sound which she thought she recognised and which she found soothing, and it lulled her to sleep. She slept. The hours passed. Eventually a key turned in the lock.

It wasn't Ron. It was the nephew person, dressed in something humans called military uniform.

"Oh, you poor thing," he said patting her. He took her outside in the garden and then he searched for her food and gave her something to eat. Then he went round the house, and he seemed to be turning a lot of switches off and checking doors and windows.

Tears in his eyes the nephew crouched down and spoke to Winnie.

"Look, Ron had a heart attack and died." He paused and patted Winnie. "So, he won't be coming back. I am in the army for at least the next six months so I am away a lot so unfortunately, I cannot keep you. I wish things were different because I know you are a great dog, and I wish I could have you. It was amazing that I happened to be in the barracks when the news came about uncle as I am off abroad again in days."

Winnie looked up at his face questioningly and gave him a paw.

"I am really sorry, but I shall have to take you to the dog rescue kennels, but I will give them a big donation to help them look after you and find you a new home." He put a lead on her and took her to his car. He seemed to be choking back tears.

Winnie was bewildered as they drove along various roads away from the bungalow and frequently whimpered. Soon they were at the kennels, and she could hear dogs barking and vaguely recognised the sounds and smells. Quickly she was placed in a kennel by strong but kindly hands. Reg did not go to see her to say 'goodbye'; if she had understood she would have realised he would have found it too upsetting. Now she waited once again for someone to be her person.

Chapter 3

School Lives

Miss Deamer had worked hard to transform the Primary Academy from a school with a somewhat poor reputation to a school with mainly happy pupils and staff and a good reputation. She was aware the buildings left something to be desired, but she believed in making the best of what she had. That had been drawn from her life experience. Her parents had fancied themselves as intellectuals being academics who were known for their poetry and philosophy. But she and her brother had enjoyed an idyllic childhood being largely allowed to roam free in the Oxfordshire countryside with their dogs Biddy and Bessie. The dogs were Golden Corgis, a glorious mix of Golden Retriever and Corgi.

These days her parents had a miniature Yorkshire terrier and had moved into a bungalow in a leafy suburb away from the open countryside and nearer to Miss Deamer's area, so close enough for Miss Deamer to visit fortnightly, if not more. They were still fairly active but had slowed down from their past habits of going to multiple poetry festivals. Her brother, Dr Dryden Deamer, was a renowned physician who had gone to the other side of the world. He was President of the Antipodean Royal Association of General Physicians. He had a wife and two children, now teenagers, but she saw nothing of this family since they were so far away in New Zealand. Her life was the school apart from her visits to her parents and time spent with Miss Dymock.

Miss Dymock was her family. They lived in a bungalow up the track next to the school sports' field. It was a pleasant enough spot, and they only had a three minute stroll to work. Miss Dymock had travelled widely in the past and walls of the bungalow were covered with ethnographica, from pictures made of banana leaves to Ashanti mask carvings. The bungalow was filled with the sound of worldwide music or the sound of Miss Dymock practicing on the piano. Yet, Miss Deamer felt there was something missing.

Miss Dymock seemed happy enough. She had her music. She had her interest in ethnographic arts. It is true she would sometimes say,

"It seems a little empty when we get home."

Cecilia Dymock was also the founder member of the local knitting club. As well as her music she had started to learn British Sign Language. Adrianne Deamer felt she should ask her what she meant by saying the bungalow felt empty when they got home.

Miss Deamer was deep in thought when she bumped into the newest member of her staff who was carrying a mop and broom.

"Sorry," said the two women at the same time.

"I think it really was my fault, Sabrina," said Miss Deamer.

Sabrina smiled nervously. She had joined the school as a part-time cleaner over a year ago, having adopted her aunt's last name of Wheeler. She generally came in after school to clean, but she also popped in at lunchtime as she was being trained up to be a lunchtime supervisor. She lived in the village with her Aunt Tracey who also cleaned at the school, the farm shop and at the village pub. After Sabrina had fled from her husband she spent about six months at a Women's Refuge. For a while she had just felt frozen with fear. Gradually after starting some counselling, she had built up the confidence to begin divorce proceedings and get back into contact with her parents.

She had spent a short time living in the parental home and her mother had tried to be kind and patient. One day her mother said,

"I am not sure this is working out… we all feel as if we are walking on eggshells when we talk to you. I have spoken to Tracey, she says you can go there for a bit."

Sabrina had been shocked.

"Are you throwing me out?" she queried.

"No," said her mum, "but you need a fresh start."

"Auntie Tracey lives in the countryside… I don't know if I can face it," said Sabrina. "And has she the room?"

"Your cousins have both left home… one got married and lives in the village. The other went to London. Your Uncle Brian is out all hours with his job on the farm. She would welcome the company. It is not the middle of nowhere, it's got a pub, the odd shop, takeaway, and it's on a bus route. It is some distance from that ghastly place. Tracey and Brian used to live in some farmworkers' cottage but now they live on a new development, so you won't feel isolated."

Sabrina had gone to bed to toss and turn that night. Somehow her dreams had been invaded by the black cat with yellow eyes saying, "Go, go." So, she had moved to Willowrose to stay with Tracey and Brian Wheeler and had then got her job at the school (enabling Tracey to concentrate more on her cleaning jobs elsewhere). She didn't have a social life outside of the family but was happy to enjoy family events with her aunt and uncle and sometimes babysat her cousin's young children. She was content with her job and pleased to be trained to be a lunchtime supervisor. Recently she had spotted a black cat walking around the edge of the school playground. He had stopped and for a fleeting second, she thought she saw those same yellow eyes she had seen before. Surely it could not be the same cat!

Miss Deamer and Sabrina spoke cordially and then Miss Deamer hurried to her office. Miss Deamer had her mind on some of her more troublesome pupils. For example, there was Nathan Clarke. Nathan tended to sit in a corner and scribbled pictures of animals rather than listen to the class. When anyone could get him to do a full picture or sketch, he showed artistic talent. His concentration was poor and had a habit of hitting out if he felt frustrated.

Being of small stature he also could be at the mercy of taller bullying pupils. She had a nasty feeling that some children teased him because he was of mixed race, his father having come from Ghana. Miss Deamer could not put her finger on it but something about Gilly Handle and Natalie Rice-Jones made her hackles rise. Tall for their ages, both with indulgent mothers who drove very upmarket cars, they had an unpleasant habit of standing around outside the doors of the school toilets. She hoped they were not making life difficult for the new girl, Leonora.

It was after school, and Sabrina found she was humming to herself as she polished the glass in the main door. A friendly but hesitant male voice said,

"Hello, erm. I have a misdelivered parcel." A tall well-proportioned man with short hair and a smiling face said, "The box is addressed to St Rita's. I am the new manager at the pub, the St Rita's Arms. The box says 'Academic Supplies' so I don't think it's for us. My barman said the school changed its name, so things are often misdelivered. I am Reg by the way." He put the parcel down and proffered a hand.

"Reg?" queried Sabrina as she put down her polishing cloth. "The Parish Mag said the new manager was a Mr Ravel Green." She wondered why Tracey had not mentioned anything about the new manager since she cleaned at the pub, but then again, she thought there was no reason to do so. Sabrina decided not to mention the connection.

"Oh," laughed Reg, "my full name is Ravel Elvis Green. My mother, bless her, is fond of music and liked that music that couple used for the skating… Ravel's Bolero… ages ago."

"Way before my time I suspect," said Sabrina.

"Well," continued Reg, "she also likes Elvis Presley, hence my name. But I was in the forces. Ravel didn't seem to fit. But my mates having got through calling me ravioli and such, noticed my initials R.E.G… so Reg I became!"

He paused. "What's your name? I recently joined civvy street, so I don't know many people."

"Sabrina," she replied. "I will take the parcel to the headteacher. Thank you for bringing it over." She smiled cautiously and disappeared into the school.

Next morning Lenny's mother Kate dropped her off fairly early at school because Kate had a meeting. Tony had left for work even earlier. The doors to the school buildings were not yet unlocked but Miss Dymock was on hand to keep an eye on things; or so she thought. While she was assisting some younger children out of a car Natalie Rice-Jones and Gilly Handle came into the playground by climbing over a side wall which was slightly more accessible since creepers gave children footholds. They immediately made for the bench where Lenny was sitting under a tree which overhung a corner of the playground.

"We don't like you," said Natalie. "You are not from round here."

"But I live at Woodland View just outside the village," replied Lenny.

"Yeah," said Gilly, "you live in the witch's house."

"And your people are strangers. Not from the village," added Natalie.

"Well, we live here now. And it's not a witch's house," replied Lenny.

"Well, you are outsiders gone into the witch's house, so I reckon you are a witch," added Gilly.

"Witch, witch, witch," Gilly and Natalie called out. They danced around her pulling faces.

"Stop being mean," cried out Lenny but Gilly snatched her lunch bag and threw it with some force upwards, so it came to rest on a tree branch.

"Fly up and get it, witch," laughed Gilly.

Lenny was on the verge of tears and at that point Nathan Clarke appeared.

"What's happened?" he queried.

"Those mean girls threw my lunch bag into the tree," said Lenny tearfully.

"I will see if I can climb up and get it," said Nathan peering up into the branches.

Natalie and Gilly were giggling and making the most of the situation and yelled, "Monkey, monkey, climb that tree," at Nathan, when suddenly there was a 'miaow' and a hiss and a black cat with amber eyes speedily climbed up the tree. He paused for just a second glowering at the two girls who had stopped laughing and whose mouths were wide open with surprise. Then with a quick flick of his paw the lunch bag was tumbling off the branches into Lenny's lap.

"Maybe she is a witch," said Gilly, "I think we should go." She headed closer to the school door with Natalie.

The black cat climbed down from the tree and rubbed himself against Lenny and Nathan purring loudly.

"Is he your cat? What's his name?" queried Nathan.

"He's not my cat… but I have seen him before, I think," said Lenny. "We got a dog a few weeks ago. She's nice. But I wish I could play with her more. Her name is Winnie."

The cat looked enigmatic and purred even louder.

"I think he is Mr Purr… kins," said Nathan.

"Mr Perkins," said Lenny. "That is a good name."

Mr Perkins walked slowly away and climbed over the wall and disappeared out of sight. A bell sounded for the start of the school day and the two children walked into the school together smiling.

Lenny was slowly getting to know the school. She was pleased to have made friends with Nathan. At breaktime she told him more about her dog and he showed her pictures he had drawn of wildlife in the area.

"They are very good," said Lenny, "I hope the teachers like them."

"Dunno," said Nathan, "I am always getting told off."

"Where do you live?" asked Lenny.

"Twelve Tree Bottom," answered Nathan. "Did you know your dad works with my dad? My dad is Christopher Clarke, the Managing Partner. And he told your dad about the house you live in… when it was for sale."

Lenny did not know what a Managing Partner was, and she was sure Nathan did not know, so she did not ask him.

"My mum trains horses," said Nathan. "Sometimes I draw them. Mum and Dad say if I don't do better at school, I will have to go away to a special boarding school. I don't want to go. I like being with animals and drawing them."

"You should come over and help me walk Winnie the dog," was all Lenny could reply.

The school day seemed to go quite quickly for Lenny and Nathan. When Lenny was collected by her mother, they rushed home to let out Winnie. She was scratching at the back door and Kate said,

"I know this back porch area needs a bit of attention, but I wish I could be home more often at lunchtime. I understand the poor dog has had a tough life."

Lenny recalled going to the rescue kennels with her mother and how Winnie had been brought out on a lead to them in a garden area. She had immediately wagged her tail and licked Lenny's face. They were told that this was her second rescue, and she had been in the kennels for nearly four months because of her history. The kennels had sent someone to checkout their home and garden and Kate claimed she would be working from home most days. Kate continued,

"I will advertise locally for a dog-walker." Lenny thought she could see the black cat looking enigmatically at them from the undergrowth.

Next morning Sabrina was at school, early, before Lenny or any of the other children since there had been a spillage of paints yesterday in the art area. She was just locking up her newly acquired second-hand bicycle, when a friendly voice said,

"Hello, it's me, more misdelivered post."

It was Reg.

"Thank you," said Sabrina, fiddling with the stiff padlock. Reg said,

"Do you need some WD40?"

"Hopefully, it's alright. I am probably not used to it. The bike is new to me. I want to be a bit more mobile."

"Sounds a good idea in this area," said Reg. "I own a fancy bike I bought for exercise when I came out of the army. But I have yet to really use it!"

Reg handed the post to Sabrina. As she took it there was a sudden, "Miaow," and the black cat appeared. He started to rub around her legs.

"Is he your cat?" asked Reg. "He is beautiful."

"No," said Sabrina, "he is very like a stray cat I knew two or three years ago. It was quite some miles from here and very different circumstances. Although I think the cat was feral, he was strangely therapeutic."

Reg looked puzzled. Sabrina said, "I was in a bad relationship. The cat always seemed to show up at an appropriate moment!"

The black cat purred loudly. "A really Mr Purr—kins," joked Reg who continued,

"My life in the forces meant I never managed family life. Some people manage it, but I am afraid I thought it was too hard on any potential wife and kids. I would have liked a dog or a cat too. But the lifestyle was not suitable. I hope I can put down roots here. First impressions are good! I was so lucky the Colonel knows the people who owned the pub, and he put in a good word for me."

He smiled. "I assume you live not far away?"

Although Sabrina was wary, she replied, "Yes, with my family the Wheelers."

"Are you related to Tracey Wheeler?" queried Reg.

"She is my aunt," was the response.

"Your aunt cleans at the pub and sometimes Brian pops in for a beer… nice people," said Reg. "You should pop in too."

"Maybe," said Sabrina. "Listen I better go and do a bit of work!"

"See you again…" said Reg as she went inside. The cat looked enigmatically up at him and purred.

He began to walk away when three young girls appeared, one on her own and two whispering together. It was Natalie and Gilly. They started to run towards the cat. Gilly picked up a clod of earth and launched it towards Mr Perkins. The cat hissed loudly and arched his back.

"Stop it, stop it, you cruel monsters, you wouldn't like stones thrown at you," shouted Lenny as she rushed to put herself between Natalie and Gilly and the cat. Reg bent down and scooped up the cat who quickly settled in his arms purring.

Miss Dymock suddenly appeared alerted by the noise. Natalie and Gilly had seemingly started to cry.

"Miss, Miss," said Gilly, "Lenny threatened to throw stones at us and called us rude words."

"Is that true?" Miss Dymock said to Lenny.

Before Lenny could answer Reg intervened, "Whoa... these little madams are putting on crocodile tears. One actually threw something at this cat." Mr Perkins made a pathetic sounding 'Miaow' as if in pain. Reg went on, "This young girl just tried to defend the cat."

"You don't want to believe him," said Natalie, "I think he works at that pub. My mum owns a beauty salon, and my dad is an accountant."

"Yeah," said Gilly, "and my mum and dad own the golf club."

"Is that so?" said Reg laughing. "But I am sure they don't want stories all over social media about how a local pub manager had to call the RSPCA out because their little girls were ill-treating a cat..."

"That will not be necessary," said Miss Dymock, "I accept what you say. Leonora go to your classroom. Gilly and Natalie please go and sit outside the Head's office and wait for me."

The children did as they were told. Reg put Mr Perkins down. The cat sat himself down and started washing himself.

"I am Reg Green, the newish manager of the pub. I just popped some misdelivered post across," said Reg.

"Thank you," said Miss Dymock. "I am sure you were not really going to call the RSPCA, but at least those two were made to think that you would! I can't abide animal cruelty. Is your cat alright?"

"He is not mine. He seems to be hanging around here. I've nicknamed him Mr Perkins. He looks okay," Reg replied. Mr Perkins purred with approval and went to sit on the playground wall. Miss Dymock went inside the school and Reg returned to the pub.

Gilly and Natalie's mothers were not pleased to be telephoned and told their children each had a 40 minute detention that day. When Lenny came out of school with the rest of the children Kate had Winnie with her in the car. Mr Perkins was nowhere to be seen, and Winnie gave Lenny joyous tail wags and licks.

"I was working from home today, so we had a long walk at lunchtime," said Kate.

Lenny tried to tell her about the incident with Gilly and Natalie and the cat, but Kate was engrossed with getting them home and then settling Winnie down again.

"By the way," said Kate almost as an afterthought, "we are having a colleague of your dad over on Sunday for lunch with his family. His lad Nathan is a classmate of yours. He likes animals I hear. I think the weather may be too cold now for anything outside, but I am sure Nathan will enjoy seeing Winnie in the garden."

Lenny was delighted to hear the news. Although she missed her old school and was worried by the actions of the two young bullies, she was pleased to have a nearby friend at her new school. When she looked out of her bedroom window, she thought she saw the black cat with the yellow eyes in the woods opposite.

Chapter 4

Winnie goes Walkies

Winnie sat in the back porch area of 'Woodland View'. She had a big dog bed, a bowl of water, a bowl of dried dog food and some dog toys. She had lived at her new home for several weeks. Most of the time she was happy, but if she was in the enclosed porch area for a long time, she worried she had been left again. She loved her new people, particularly the youngest one, Lenny. She felt attached to Kate as well and tried to please Tony, who sometimes played ball with her.

When she had returned to the rescue kennels, she had not understood why she was there and for the first few weeks she had barely eaten anything. The kennel maids had tried to give her special attention and had coaxed her to eat. She began eating and enjoyed their attention. They had tried to introduce her to people but somehow, they just didn't seem right so she would just turn her back on them.

One day there were voices in the corridor outside her kennels. The kennel maid said, "She is rather shy and sad. Her previous owner died so she may not come out for you."

She saw the man, the woman and the child for the first time but just lay with her head between her paws.

"Please can I go in and stroke her?" said the child. Before the kennel maid could say either way, Lenny had gone in on her hands and knees.

"I was about to say, it would be safer if I brought her out."

By then Lenny had lain down next to the dog and was stroking the dog and whispering to her,

"Please be my friend, I don't have any friends here yet."

The kennel maid quickly brought her outside and there was much tail wagging.

Tony said, "We only moved to the area about 2 weeks ago. Lenny misses her old friends."

Winnie raised her head and licked Lenny's face. Dog and child had an immediate bond. Gradually introductions were made to Kate and Tony. When Winnie came back to the house there was a lot of bouncing and tail wagging. She raced around the garden. She licked each of her new family in turn. She played ball excitedly with Tony.

Tony said, "Until she is fully settled in, she better stay in the old porch if there is no-one at home."

When everyone was at home Winnie loved her people and her home. She enjoyed her walks with Kate, occasional catch games with Tony and the company of Lenny. She even slept on the end of Lenny's bed, but Winnie worried when she was shut up in the porch for what felt like a long time. She was generally a well-behaved dog except she hated to be left shut in what seemed to her a small space and without knowledge her people might return, so she often howled and scratched on the door.

Lenny and Nathan did their best to avoid the attention of the two bullies Gilly and Natalie. They sat the other side of the playground to avoid their arrival. However, when the two girls arrived, they made straight for Lenny and Nathan. Gilly started by mocking Nathan,

"My mum says you shouldn't have been allowed in this country, monkeyface."

"I was born here," he answered. "I don't call you names even though I could."

Gilly said, "Maybe it's cos you are too stupid."

"Stupid monkey," joined in Natalie.

Nathan got up as if to hit the girls, making fists at them. Lenny got up quickly and stood between them.

"Look you pair of nasties; we are all descended from animals. A man called Charles Darwin says so. The way you talk… it's just horrid," said Lenny.

"Witch, witch," the two bullies screamed at Lenny.

"If I had the power of a magic witch, I would call for that cat to come and scratch you," said Lenny.

At that moment there was a loud, "Miaow," and Mr Perkins charged out of a nearby bush. His tail flicked from side to side. Then he arched his back and hissed loudly at Gilly and Natalie. They quickly retreated and he rubbed himself against Lenny and Nathan purring.

"Gosh," said Nathan, "that was odd… but good."

"Thank you, Mr Perkins," said Lenny.

Mr Perkins looked up at the children and said, "Miaow," and was gone.

Lenny and Nathan sat next to each other in class. Some of the lessons were very dull. To her surprise Miss Dymock made an announcement at the beginning of the school day,

"Today, children, Years 4, 5 and 6 are going to have a special lesson on what it was like in the olden days to go to school in this village. Miss Lavinia Lupin used to teach at this school, and she also has a special interest in the history of education in Victorian times. She will give us a short talk about what this school was like in the nineteen sixties. She will then give us a presentation on what it was like for Victorian school children. I will be helping her display some slides which I am sure you will find very interesting. Each of your year groups will then have projects about school and childhood. Year 4, you will take the subject of 'inside a Victorian classroom', Year 5 you will take the subject of 'being a child in the nineteen sixties' and Year 6 you will take the subject 'how things for children have changed since Victorian days'.

Lenny was surprised when Aunt Lavinia entered the room and stood next to Miss Dymock. She had seen Aunt Lavinia twice since her family had moved house. A few days after the move Mum and Dad and herself had endured another of Aunt Lavinia's appalling afternoon teas. Then a couple of weeks ago Mum had fetched Aunt Lavinia to 'Woodland View'. She had been given a tour of the house and then given tea and biscuits in the conservatory. The highlight for Aunt Lavinia had been meeting Winnie.

Winnie seemed to sense that Aunt Lavinia was elderly and therefore was on her best behaviour. She sat next to Aunt Lavinia wagging her tail and being intermittently patted by her new fan.

"Oh, you beautiful girl," said Aunt Lavinia to the dog. "I do so miss my Dickie."

She looked wistful and added, "I couldn't take a dog for a walk these days, with my bad legs."

Indeed, Lenny wondered how Aunt Lavinia was going to manage in the classroom. She also wondered why Aunt Lavinia had never mentioned her connection with the school.

Aunt Lavinia said in ringing tones, "Where am I supposed to sit?"

Miss Dymock reacted and replied, "Right, four volunteers to bring that big office chair from the Head's office."

Lenny and Nathan put their hands up and were chosen with two other children to fetch the chair. Aunt Lavinia smiled at Lenny as she went past.

When the chair was put into position Miss Dymock adjusted some knobs to raise the height of the seat.

"Too low!" said Aunt Lavinia in ringing tones.

"It's as high as I can make it," responded an exasperated Miss Dymock.

Lenny put her hand up.

"What?" asked Miss Dymock sounding annoyed.

"Miss, I can get some cushions from the floor of the library area," answered Lenny.

Miss Dymock smiled gratefully and sent her to get some cushions from the area where younger children had story time and older children had supported reading if needed. Aunt Lavinia smiled at Lenny as she passed her.

Eventually the chair was as Aunt Lavinia wished it and with the assistance of Miss Dymock and Lenny, she climbed up into it. She paused and looked down at the children and said,

"That's better. Now I can start. I always used to sit on a tall seat when I taught here. It meant I could see all the children, even when I was sitting down. There was no messing about at the back of the classroom. If children misbehaved, I could stop them immediately. I would call them out to the front of the class and make them go and stand in a corner. If I thought they were very naughty I would make them stand on a chair with a sign on them such as 'dunce' or 'disobedient' for the morning and even smack them across the hands with a ruler… wouldn't be allowed now."

She paused,

"Every mid-morning class would stop for milk. Little bottles of milk were delivered by a milkman to the school. We don't have a milkman in the village now. In the nineteen sixties it was usual in towns for milkmen to deliver milk to houses in an electric truck called a milk float. In the early sixties the village milkman still used a horse and cart to bring milk to the school. Although milk was good for the pupils, they used to moan a lot about having to drink it. The trouble was there was nowhere to store it, so the crates just sat in the playground and the milk got frozen in the winter and went bad in the summer."

She continued,

"Another thing which was frozen in the winter were the toilets. There are more buildings here now than when I first came to the school. When I first started teaching there was just the main Victorian building. The toilets were in a basic outhouse at the corner of the playground. They had the old metal cisterns with chains for the flush and basic basins with cold water to rinse your hands. They were totally unheated. My recollection is that there was no electric light in there, either, so the only light was from some rudimentary windows high on the wall. The toilets and basins often froze solid in the winter."

Leonora shivered at the thought of it.

"People didn't know any different," said Aunt Lavinia. "Mind you the nineteen sixties were times of great change. Young grown-up people began to listen to pop and rock music a great deal… except a few of us. I stuck with Classical music."

Aunt Lavinia continued to talk about the nineteen sixties and how excited the children had been when the first man had visited the moon.

"We had a big television in the hall on the Monday morning," she said. "Mind you the screens were small by today's standards. The landing had been going on overnight. Children saw some of the broadcast on the Monday morning and they also repeated the film. That was a good, exciting thing of that era, seeing an American astronaut walk on the moon. I think that people thought that by now we would all be able to visit the moon!"

Miss Dymock was doing her best to do a bit of signing to supplement the talk for a couple of children who were hearing impaired. Some of the other children were not concentrating as well as Lenny and Nathan and soon there was a big distraction.

Winnie had been howling and scratching at the door of the porch. Lenny was at school. Tony had left for the office quite early, and after Kate had dropped Lenny at school she had carried on to the office. The door to the outside seemed to rattle a lot and was not of the firm double glazed construction of the inner door. After a while, a voice said, "Miaow," to Winnie. A paw seemed to hook itself into a little gap which had developed between the outer door and the frame. The cat appeared to pull at the door with his paw and Winnie started pushing the door with her nose. They appeared to work together for some time and then the door burst open, and Winnie was free.

She stood there and sniffed, apparently trying to pick up the scent of her people.

"Miaow," said Mr Perkins and then rubbed himself against Winnie. He walked a few steps along the garden path, tail erect, and stopped. Winnie followed and stopped beside him. Mr Perkins led her outside of the garden and Winnie followed. Soon the cat was leading the dog along the verge beside the lane in the direction of the village. It was not long before they arrived at the school, and he led her into the school playground.

Winnie was sure she could smell one of her people and wagged her tail with excitement. Mr Perkins led her to a double door. She caught a glimpse of Lenny and pushed the doors and burst into the room. Woofing with delight she bounded up to Lenny.

"Winnie, whatever are you doing here?" exclaimed Lennie as pandemonium ensued.

Children were laughing, Winnie was barking. Miss Dymock and Aunt Lavinia were looking surprised. Miss Deamer appeared having heard the noise followed by Sabrina who had come to take a turn as a lunchtime supervisor.

Winnie seemed to quieten down and was trying to lick Lenny's face.

"Please, Miss Dymock," she said, "I am so sorry. It's my dog. I don't know how she has got out."

"Well, she can't stay here! We will have to call one of your parents and in the meantime, she will have to wait in a more suitable place, maybe a storeroom," responded Miss Dymock.

Lenny guided the excited dog through the excited children towards the adults.

"Aren't you beautiful!" said Aunt Lavinia who seemed uncertain if she recognised Winnie or not. "Rather bigger than my Dickie was, but a beautiful doggy nonetheless."

"Mum's at the office," said Lenny as Aunt Lavinia and Miss Deamer both began to stroke the dog. "I don't know what to do because I think she will be ages. She is not due back to the village until 3.15 to collect me."

"She's a bit big for me to handle or I would take her to my cottage," said Aunt Lavinia.

Sabrina stepped out of the shadows. Winnie looked up at her questioningly; wasn't this the person who had been kind to her when she had been in a bad place?

"She looks so like a dog I used to know. Maybe I can help?" said Sabrina. "But I think we need a lead or something to attach to her collar."

"I still have Dickie's lead in my cottage. I couldn't bear to part with it when he died. If you could help me off the chair, maybe someone could help me go and fetch it," contributed Aunt Lavinia.

Nathan volunteered to assist. He walked alongside Aunt Lavinia as she hobbled to her cottage and then ran back at speed with the lead as she lagged behind.

Sabrina assisted Lenny putting Winnie on a lead.

"Why don't I take the dog for a walk and then sit with her somewhere until Lenny's mother collects her," suggested Sabrina. "I was only assisting at lunchtime so I am sure they can manage without me."

"She is a nice looking dog," said Miss Dymock. "That is a plan of sorts. I hope your mother makes sure your dog is secure in the future, Lenny."

Miss Deamer said, "She seems a nice natured dog, so I don't mind if she waits in the office part of the time with Sabrina. Is it okay with you, Lenny?"

Winnie was now enjoying tummy rubs from Sabrina and Nathan.

"I think so," said Lenny.

Aunt Lavinia reappeared. "Victorian school after lunch break," she said somewhat randomly.

Sabrina coaxed Winnie out of the room and soon they were outside. Lenny followed them outside, seemingly a little reluctant to have her dog walked by the school dinner lady.

"You are such a nice dog," said Sabrina. "What did they say your name was?"

"It's Winnie," said Lenny.

"That's amazing," said Sabrina. "Must be well over two years ago I knew a lovely young dog called Winnie. I was in a bad place, and I couldn't help her… I heard she was taken into the rescue kennels. I always hoped she would go to a good home. I am so pleased you have her. How long ago did she start living with you?"

"Not that long, maybe about two months ago," replied Lenny. "We got her from the rescue kennels. They said her previous owner had died in the hot weather."

"Maybe she is not the same dog, but she seems to like me. I promise I will take care of her when I walk her and then she can go home with you and your mum," responded Sabrina.

With some reluctance Lenny went back inside. Sabrina and Winnie greatly enjoyed their walk. There was a lot of tail wagging and sniffing. Meanwhile, Lenny found it hard to enjoy her lunch. Nathan tried to reassure her, but she could see Gilly and Natalie staring at her and giggling. Aunt Lavinia's talk on Victorian school life was very interesting too, but she still felt nervous.

By the end of the school day when Lenny's mother came to collect her, Sabrina was sitting quietly in Miss Deamer's office with Winnie. Kate was rather surprised when both Aunt Lavinia and Miss Dymock approached her car.

"Is Lenny alright?" she asked.

Miss Dymock and Aunt Lavinia gave her a summary of what had happened.

Kate started to apologise to Miss Dymock when Lenny came bouncing out of the school closely followed by Miss Deamer, Sabrina and Winnie.

Kate began to apologise again. Miss Deamer and Sabrina were smiling broadly.

Sabrina said, "I did enjoy walking Winnie. She is so like a dog called Winnie I used to know."

Miss Deamer added, "A lovely dog, makes me wonder why I don't have one."

Aunt Lavinia suggested she saw the family again soon. Lenny did not look forward to her aunt's sandwiches but had warmed to her a little more today.

There were smiles all round. Then they made their 'goodbyes'. Kate bundled Lenny and Winnie into her car and drove the short distance home.

Nobody looked at the black cat sitting on the wall of the playground with a self-satisfied look to his face. Mr Perkins blinked his enigmatic yellow eyes and then he jumped down and disappeared into the shadows under the trees.

Chapter 5

Of Fields and Bicycles

The man called Kenny had served time in prison for animal cruelty offences, possessive and coercive control of Sabrina, resisting arrest and illegal gambling offences. He was out of prison on licence and had been for a while. He had not gone back to his ramshackle former property. He had only been out hare coursing once and was anxious not to let his probation officer know what he was doing these days. He told his probation officer he was employed as a warehouseman, and the officer was gullible enough to swallow the story backed up with dubious paperwork and fake emails. He had looked out over the fields from the warehouse where he was sitting and decided that while other criminal activities were preferable for him these days, there was one person from his past he wished to find. As he sat filing off serial numbers from a shotgun and looking at the lucrative boxes of illegal weapons and packs of drugs in his new storeroom, he made plans to find Sabrina and exact his revenge.

Other people were thinking about Sabrina at this time, but in a positive light. Kate was talking to Tony,

"I was wondering about asking the dinner lady who looked after Winnie when she got out, if she could manage the dog walking job. So far, I have only had two applicants for the job. One was a young kid of about 13 and I felt he was too young. The other applicant was from some distance away... she is a professional animal sitter, but she wanted me to leave Winnie with her all day because of the travelling. "

Tony replied, "Well, you could ask the dinner lady if she could fit it in... but she would need to be able to reach our house which is a little way out of town, and we would probably need a reference off the school... and she would have to want the job!"

As it happened Sabrina had been thinking of Winnie too. She had seen the advertisement for a dog walker and had been thinking about whether she had the time to fit in the job. When Kate came to collect Lenny from school, she lingered a little while to see if she could see Sabrina. Winnie was in the back of the car. After her escape from the porch, she now had the run of the kitchen and hallway of the house which Winnie found much less stressful. However, Kate was keen she had a walk in the daytime on days she went to the office and to court.

Kate, Lenny and Winnie sat with the car windows slightly open as most of the other children left. Suddenly, Winnie started to bark and wag her tail. Sabrina arrived on her bicycle. Kate got out of the car and the two women greeted each other cheerfully.

"I don't supervise lunch every day at school," explained Sabrina. "On days when I do supervise lunch, I would be able to cycle down just after, about 2, if that would be okay? Some days it could be earlier. I pop into the school each afternoon for a couple of hours after the kids have finished, and now and again I clean first thing before school, so there would be time to walk Winnie."

An agreement was soon reached and on days when Kate could not walk Winnie herself, Sabrina would be propelled along by Winnie on her lead across footpaths through the local fields and woods.

Winnie and Lenny were both much happier. On the weekend when Christopher Clarke and his wife Deena brought Nathan to 'Woodland View' for Sunday lunch, Nathan and Lenny put on coats and played joyous games of catch around the garden with Winnie. Winnie sat at the children's side as Lenny introduced Nathan to Midge and Mabel the guinea pigs.

On the other side of the terrace Tony and Christopher sat on a garden bench enjoying post lunch cigars.

"I don't think the ladies really want us to smoke cigars, let alone have them in the house," said Tony.

"I know, and it is not really good for us… but hey, once in a blue moon as a treat!" answered Christopher.

The two men talked about their office and matters in the news and then Tony said,

"I am surprised you don't have a dog for Nathan, I mean wouldn't one live around your wife's stables?"

Christopher puffed on his cigar and responded, "Deena had two dogs, Springer spaniels, when she was younger. They got old and died when Nathan was a baby. She trains racehorses and as Nathan is a bit of a challenge said that she couldn't manage to train racehorses, a dog and a child."

Tony persisted, "Winnie has made so much difference to Lenny. Maybe a pet of his own would help Nathan. He seems to really love animals."

"I will give it some thought," said Christopher without commitment.

Tony then changed the subject.

"Did you know my old great aunt Lavinia Lupin gave a talk to the children at school? She used to teach there."

"I heard about the old lady's interesting talk, but I hadn't realised she was related to you," replied Christopher. "In the village where I lived in Ghana as a child, we generally called older women 'auntie' as a mark of respect."

"Well, it seems that Aunt Lavinia and others need some legal help to do with the school," said Tony, "and I don't know which of us should oblige."

Tony explained that the big playing field behind the school was not actually school property. It was owned by a Charitable Trust called the 'Willowrose Active Recreational Trust' (otherwise known as 'Wart'). From what Aunt Lavinia said some previous Trustees had died and the ownership of the field had never been properly registered, indeed the deeds were probably lost.

Christopher laughed. "That sounds a horrible mess which I would prefer to avoid. However, with a kid at the school and a need to try to get accepted by a few of the locals because they are suspicious of the colour of my skin, I suppose I better volunteer!"

"I might come with you for the first meeting, to show willing," added Tony.

There was a rustling in the bushes and Mr Perkins came sauntering out and rubbed himself around the legs of Tony and Christopher, purring.

"What a superb cat," said Christopher. "Yours?"

"No," said Tony, "he just seems to hang around locally."

"You know," said Christopher, "I wouldn't mind a cat."

Mr Perkins purred as if he approved and rubbed and gave Christopher a knowing look before he disappeared into the bushes.

On Monday Christopher and Tony took steps to arrange a meeting. Sabrina was not required for dog walking that Monday so that at quarter to two she unlocked her bicycle intending to go home. She had only gone a few yards when another vaguely familiar person came into view. It was Reg on his racing cycle. He was not sporting Lycra but did have a helmet and a short high visibility waistcoat over ordinary casual clothes. He wobbled a bit and came to a stop calling,

"Whoa… Hello."

Sabrina stopped as well. They both pulled their bicycles off the road.

"I am not doing very well," said Reg.

Sabrina laughed and said, "I don't suppose you had to ride a bike in the army."

"Nope," said Reg. "I thought I should get some exercise, Monday is actually my day off, because the pub doesn't open until 6.30 in the evening on Mondays."

He continued, "I don't suppose you could ride with me for a bit to give me confidence?"

"OK, just a short way, maybe as far as the farm shop," said Sabrina reluctantly.

They remounted their cycles and with Sabrina in the lead soon reached the farm shop.

"Are you free to go any further?" queried Reg. "It's okay if you are not."

In the event they cycled as far as Twelve Tree Bottom, a hamlet which had half a dozen houses, some smart stables, and the driveway to the local stately home 'Bluffington Hall'.

Reg said, "My colonel grew up there. I understand the Bluffingtons were the local gentry in these parts and still own a lot of land here."

"Yes," said Sabrina, "Uncle Brian works on Bluffington Farm. He combines managing their rare breed pig programme with being a gamekeeper."

Reg said, "I am glad I cycled this far. Thank you for your help. I don't want to impose on you further so I think we should turn round. Can I buy you a coffee at the farm shop?"

Sabrina said, "Thank you. Maybe another time."

They cycled back to the village and stopped outside the pub.

"Would you cycle with me another Monday?" asked Reg.

"I am not sure," said Sabrina, "I do dog walking on some days now."

Reg did not press the point. On Wednesday he decided to take a very short ride after the lunchtime crowd had gone, but before he had to prepare for the evening. He only took himself as far as the entrance to a public footpath just after the farm shop. As he paused to turn round Sabrina and Winnie came bowling along the footpath. Winnie wagged her tail and bounced excitedly. Reg leant his bike against a fence and began fussing the dog.

"It can't be? It's Winnie... Uncle Ron's old dog. Oh, do you have a new home now?" he said fussing Winnie.

"Yes," said Sabrina with interest, "she lives with a family just outside the village who adopted her quite recently. She is really attached to their little girl, but she needs dog walking about twice a week. Her name is indeed Winnie… But she reminds me of another Winnie. Now I am going to ask if you have time for a coffee?"

Reg said, "Maybe half an hour. I will pop in and buy us a couple of coffees, and we best sit in the garden with Winnie."

They sat there in their coats with Winnie, and Reg explained about Uncle Ron's death and how he had been unable to take on Winnie.

"Where did your Uncle Ron get Winnie from?" asked Sabrina.

"Why the same kennels to which I took her." He mentioned the location and continued, "The kennels had her after she had been rescued from somewhere in a police operation. She was quite young, I think."

Sabrina drew in a deep breath.

"I think she is the same dog called Winnie I knew over two to three years ago," she said to a surprised Reg, and continued, "I made a terrible mistake. I made a bad marriage to a violent criminal. Me and the dogs were basically his prisoners, but I managed to escape and report him for the awful things I knew about. I hope he never finds me as I still fear him."

Reg responded, "I am so sorry. I am pleased there was a happy ending for Winnie, but I understand why you were previously hesitant about having coffee with me. I won't press you any more… if you want to do a little cycling or talk to me, it will be entirely up to you."

"Thank you," said Sabrina, "I better take Winnie home now." She took the dog and waved to Reg as they turned to return across the fields.

Reg started to put his cycle helmet on when he felt as if he was being watched. Walking through a gap in the hedge was the black cat with the yellow eyes. He began rubbing himself around Reg's legs purring loudly. Reg bent down and stroked him, and said,

"You look so knowing. What is it you know that I don't?" The cat just blinked, and, in a few seconds, he was gone.

Whereas the next day Thursday turned out to be a routine day for Reg and Sabrina, Christopher and Tony freely admitted that going to the Trustee meeting of Wart seemed anything but routine. The meeting was early evening at the sports' field in question. Tony had not realised that there was a pavilion of sorts tucked away at the bottom of the field. Since the nights were drawing in, he found himself stumbling down the field with Christopher by torchlight towards a dimly lit building in the middle distance.

If asked to describe the building, he might have found it quite hard to do so. One end of it might be described as an elaborate Victorian shed but that was not even quite accurate. It was one small room with a fireplace and built in cupboards each side. On top of one of the cupboards was a Victorian era writing box with a key in its lock.

There was a table and chairs in the middle and one light bulb dangled down. There was one window in the wall opposite the fireplace. Entrance was through a heavy wooden door but at the other end of the room someone had knocked through a doorway and a wooden structure had been added which housed a small changing room. There were pegs on the wall and narrow wooden benches under the line of pegs. There was a toilet cubicle in the corner. The old fashioned cistern sat high above the partition wall with its chain dangling.

Christopher and Tony stumbled through the front door of the pavilion. It was clear the other people attending the meeting had arrived in advance. Both men recognised Miss Deamer and Miss Dymock from the school. Tony was warmly greeted by Aunt Lavinia who was seated at the table, upon which there was a notebook and fountain pen which he assumed she was using to make some sort of record of the meeting. A man with a pink face and sandy hair, clad in hunting gear, introduced himself,

"Brian Wheeler, gamekeeper, I am sorry about the clothes. I was just out doing some pest control near the pheasant enclosures."

Lurching out of the shadows from the wooden extension was a tall gangly slightly hunched figure,

"Ahh, General," said Miss Deamer. "Did the plumbing work?" as there was a gurgling clanking noise in the background.

"My plumbing is fine don't you know… but I would say the pavilion's plumbing works after a fashion, don't you know!" was the reply, but then he turned to Tony and Christopher. "Bluffington is the name, Bluffington of Bluffington Hall! General Arthur Bluffington, very much retired. And you two must be those lawyer fellows!"

Tony and Christopher could see that he too was wearing country tweeds. He had an enormous grey wispy droopy moustache. His hair was grey, wavy and flowing, worn at a length which would never have done for the army. He seemed to take control.

"Why don't we all sit down. Let us start by me introducing everyone and telling you the background," he addressed Tony and Christopher. "Miss Deamer and Miss Dymock are of course Head and Deputy Head at the School. Lavinia Lupin used to teach there, and I think may be related to one of you. Brian here works on the farm, and he is also my head gamekeeper. The five of us either are Trustees of Wart… or want to be…"

Christopher smiled and said, "Well Tony and I are both partners of Rinewater Standing, solicitors, a leading law firm. We both have children at the school. Tony lives just on the edge of the village. I live at Twelve Tree Bottom, in the house next to the stables, which my wife runs. Tony and his family have only recently moved to the village. I have spent so much time with the firm that I don't really know people in the village. We are both keen to be more involved with the village so we would like to help if we can so, please give us the history."

The general cleared his throat and responded, "My family are military men. My son is a colonel. However, over the generations we come home to Bluffington Hall, and we like to help the community. In Victorian times when the Bluffingtons still had big families one Bluffington son would run the estates, one would go into the army, one would become a vicar, one would go into the navy, and one would run for Parliament. The women would just be married off… So, there was a vicar of St Rita's who was called Eustace Bluffington. He took a great interest in the welfare of his parishioners and the school. He thought both the children and adults needed a sports' field, so he persuaded his father General Horace Bluffington to transfer to a Trust for their benefit, with himself and the then Headmaster as

Trustees for the field. Eventually the Wart Charitable Trust was set up and everyone assumed the field had been conveyed to the charity."

The general paused and cleared his throat again. "It seems the land has not been registered at the Land Registry and as yet we cannot find the deeds. We looked in the school office, and they are not there. The old vicarage was long since demolished and the vicar comes out from another parish these days. Those cupboards seem to hold old cricket stuff, and the wooden box above doesn't contain them."

"So," asked Tony, "is it an issue of lost deeds then, because there are ways of dealing with it and still getting the Trust's title registered at the Land Registry?"

"If only that were the only problem," said the general. "The loss of the deeds came to light when we wanted to appoint a new Trustee, Brian here. You see we cannot find a decent copy of the Wart Trust deed and the deed appointing the present Trustees. All we have is this!"

The general leant down and pulled some horribly shredded papers out of a box under the table.

Tony and Christopher sat down at the table. They carefully studied the papers which they laid out across the flat surface. There were parts of pages missing and there was an appalling stench of mouse droppings from the pages which lay there. Tony opened the window slightly. Christopher cleared his throat,

"Look," he said, "all may not be lost. This is a registered charity so the starting point must be to get a copy of the Charitable Deeds from the Charity Commission," and he added jokingly, "and maybe get a cat for this pavilion!"

There was a loud, "Miaow," and Mr Perkins squeezed in through the open window and sat himself in the middle of the room as if taking over chairing the meeting.

Chapter 6

Charity Begins with Perkins

When Mr Perkins sat himself down in the middle of the Wart meeting, the general initially looked astonished.

"Where on earth did that come from?" He pointed at Mr Perkins.

"Looks a nice cat. Maybe it's the one my niece mentioned was hanging around," said Brian Wheeler.

"Miaow," said Mr Perkins looking enigmatic and not moving.

Tony and Christopher laughed, and Tony said, "He definitely seems to be hanging about the area!"

"Yes, he does," said Miss Deamer.

"He is very handsome," said Aunt Lavinia. Mr Perkins purred and got up. He walked over, and she began stroking him, saying, "Your fur is very soft."

He appeared to look into her eyes.

"What about the meeting?" barked the general.

Mr Perkins placed himself in the middle of the table on top of the papers and said, "Miaow," again.

"I think it's nearly over," said Christopher, "I was suggesting making some enquiries at the Charity Commission."

"But what about the land… the deeds…?" retorted the general.

"There are ways one can deal with matters when deeds get lost although the situation is far from ideal," responded Tony.

"I want that thing out of here," said the general pointing at Mr Perkins as if he had not been listening, and Mr Perkins hissed in reply.

The general raised his hand as if to take a swipe at the cat who promptly swiped back embedding his claws in the general's hand.

"Ouch," said the general as he pulled his hand away, "he has wounded me." A trickle of blood ran out of a scratch on one hand. The general picked up Aunt Lavinia's pen and threw it at Mr Perkins.

There was a look of rage in the cat's eyes and the other members of the meeting looked variously surprised or horrified.

"Miaow," said Mr Perkins and jumped away landing on top of one of the cupboards and upsetting the old box.

The heavy wooden box seemed to hover on the edge of the cupboard before it came crashing to the floor. As it went crashing down something seemed to spring open in its bottom.

"A secret drawer!" said Miss Deamer and Miss Dymock in unison.

Aunt Lavinia bent down. There was a fat old envelope in it. She picked it up and read the handwritten words off the envelope: 'St Rita's Field Abstract of Title and Deed'.

Christopher said laughing, "Maybe there are some title deeds after all."

The general looked at Mr Perkins. "Maybe that blasted cat has found the missing title deeds!"

Mr Perkins looked enigmatic while Christopher and Tony took a brief look at the contents of the envelope.

"It seems very promising," said Tony, "but we will have to look at them more thoroughly just to be sure. Perhaps the cat should be thanked."

Aunt Lavinia said, "I have always been a dog person, but he does seem very fine and if you got scratched, General, I think it was your own fault."

The general looked slightly embarrassed and to no-one in particular said, "Sorry, sorry, sorry."

Mr Perkins jumped down off the cupboard and went straight up to the general purring.

"I guess I deserved to be scratched," said the general peering down at the cat.

"Miaow," said Mr Perkins who then made for the window and was gone.

The meeting broke up in good cheer. They agreed to meet again when Tony and Christopher had looked at the documents and made enquiries of the Charity Commission.

Miss Deamer and Miss Dymock could not help commenting on the cat to each other, the following day. Sabrina overheard them. She said,

"That black cat has been around here quite a bit. I think he is lucky. He has a tremendous purr."

"Mr Purr… kins!" joked Miss Dymock, before going to oversee Lenny's year group who were working on their projects.

Nathan and Lenny were quite enjoying working on the project they had been given 'Modern school food v Victorian school eating habits'. They were working with two other boys, and two other girls and tentative friendships were underway. One girl, Maisie, was hearing impaired and had suffered taunting by Gilly Handle and Natalie Rice-Jones in the past. The nasty little pair would stand in front of her and mouth insults such as 'Dummy' and 'Earwax'. Thankfully, Gilly and Natalie were in a different group with the subject 'Modern tech at school v Victorian written work'. Gilly and Natalie had scowled and moaned a little when being given this assignment.

"But Miss," moaned Natalie, "can't we do the one on clothes… please?"

Miss Dymock had been unimpressed and so they were working reluctantly with four other children who she actually felt were more tech-savvy than the reluctant pair. The two troublemakers were looking sullen and grumpy. She could not put her finger on it, but she was sure they were up to something. Recently children had complained of their breaktime snacks going missing causing tears on Maisie's part. The contents of Maisie's lunchbox had completely disappeared the other day. Miss Dymock could prove nothing but had her suspicions. She peered from over the top of the lectern left from Lavinia Lupin's visit and looked at the children who were mostly engrossed with their work.

As Gilly passed Lenny and Nathan's group she mouthed "witch," at Lenny and trod on the back of Lenny's shoe, catching Lenny's heel.

"Ouch, ow, ow," cried Lenny.

Immediately, Gilly called out to Miss Dymock, "Please, Miss, Lenny called me a cow."

"I didn't," said Lenny hopping with pain and with tears in her eyes.

"She didn't call her anything," said the other children in her group, "Gilly stood on her foot."

"Back to your seats," said Miss Dymock. "Stick to your own groups."

As the class drew to a close, Miss Dymock went round the class inspecting the project work. She singled out Nathan's artwork for particular praise.

"Well done," she said, "we can carry on next week. Nathan, the drawings are particularly good."

Natalie and Gilly looked livid and were whispering to each other conspiratorially.

Meanwhile at Rinewater Standing, solicitors, Christopher was pleased to note that when he examined the documents from the secret drawer, they established title to the field. When he eventually obtained documents from the Charity Commission the papers were not in such good order. The copy documents came with a disclaimer from the Commission. There was a copy of the original Wart Trust Deed and there were various deeds showing appointments and resignations of Trustees. Certainly, the general had been properly appointed Trustee. There was then a document headed 'Updated Deed of Variation and Appointment of New Trustees'. In it the general and the Trustees of that time should have signed the document to appoint Miss Deamer, Miss Dymock and Lavinia Lupin as Trustees. In the place for each signature there was just what appeared to be pencil signature in each place saying, 'A SIGNATURE'. Amongst the fragments of the original mouse-eaten documents there had been a small removable sticker with words written on it 'Sign where indicated 'A Signature'.' The only signatures were the pencilled words.

Christopher called into Tony's office and showed him.

"I might have known that old general would make a mess," laughed Tony. "I think the cat could have done a better job."

Christopher chuckled and said that he had been thinking of letting his son have a cat.

They laughed but both agreed there was a solution and quickly contacted Miss Deamer to hastily convene a meeting. They returned to the little pavilion that night with the documents lying on the table again. The general, Miss Deamer and Miss Dymock, Lavinia Lupin and Brian Wheeler looked at them anxiously. Mr Perkins had followed them into the building and sat himself at Christopher's feet.

"The good news is that as a result of the cat's actions we have enough of the deeds to be able to register title of the field at the Land Registry so everyone will know that Wart owns the field." He paused. "But there is a complication we can fix."

Christopher cleared his throat and asked the general, "General, why was the deed appointing Miss Deamer, Miss Dymock and Miss Lupin not signed by you or anyone else?"

"It was," said the general puffing out his chest and picking up the offending document, "we had a Trustees meeting and agreed the matter and I told some solicitor fellow to sort it which he did."

"Miaow," said Mr Perkins as if to disagree.

"Look," said the general pointing to the document, "see it is signed 'A Signature' by each name. It is signed."

Tony felt like hitting his head on the table. How could anyone be that stupid? He hoped the general had not been in charge of anything too important in the army.

"That is just to show people where to sign," he said with a sigh. "But fortunately we have a way forward. I won't bore you with the details, but we can draw up some further documentation and it can be properly signed and witnessed, and everything will be put right."

"Miaow," said Mr Perkins, as if to approve the proposal.

"I see that cat is here again," said the general as if to deflect. "Hopefully he can bring us luck."

"We can use a black cat logo as a symbol for the trust," contributed Brian Wheeler who had been quiet up until now. "It might detract from the awful name 'Wart' and perhaps we might just think of referring to it as the Willowrose Trust informally in the future. It might help with things like fundraising."

Mr Perkins purred loudly. The general offered to buy everyone a drink at the pub. People collected their belongings and headed to the door. Mr Perkins walked out with Christopher and Tony and then disappeared into the darkness.

The next school day saw the continuation of the projects after an initial hour of the children undertaking sums. Gilly and Natalie appeared to be missing. Lenny hoped they would not be in school at all. However, both of them sauntered in after the children had finished their calculations.

"Sorry we are late," said Gilly, "my mum's car wouldn't start."

"And your mum's car?" asked Miss Dymock of Natalie.

"It had a flat tyre," she said slightly smirking.

Miss Dymock thought she would enquire of the mothers later on. She didn't believe a word those girls said.

"Now, children. Please get out your project work from the folders," she instructed the class.

Just as she was going to speak to each individual group another member of staff appeared and said, "There has been a break in at the art cupboards."

Miss Dymock sighed. She did not want to leave the children unattended, so she asked the other teacher to watch the children from the doorway while she went to inspect and if need be, to inform Miss Deamer. Running up the corridor she caught a glimpse of the black cat with the yellow eyes sitting just outside the school. When she reached the art cupboards, she was relieved to see that the door of one of the lower cupboards only had been forced. It was used to store poster paints and marker pens. It appeared that a handful of marker pens and a few pots of paint were missing; the reds were rather depleted. On the floor was a metal ruler which had clearly been used to force open the cupboard. She made a mental note to ask Sabrina to clear up after school. She briefly called in to the office where Miss Deamer was working, on her way back to the classroom.

"I hardly think we can call the police about the theft of three or four marker pens and half a dozen pots of poster paint," she said. "Also I suspect, sadly, it is a child or children who may be the culprits."

Miss Deamer responded, "Any suspects?"

"I have no evidence," responded Miss Dymock, "but Gilly Handle and Natalie Rice-Jones were late, and I suspect their reasons were lies. However, I don't know why they would want marker pens and poster paint."

She hurried back to the classroom, having agreed with Miss Deamer that they would look into matters further later on.

When she got back to the classroom, she soon became aware that all was not well. The staff member who was supposed to keep an eye on things was not there and had apparently been called away by an urgent phone call.

Lenny and Nathan's group seemed all to be upset. Lenny and Maisie were crying. Nathan was stamping his feet and walking round in circles.

"How could they do it! How could they do it!" he was shouting in the direction of Gilly and Natalie who just looked smug.

"They scribbled on our work... they have ruined our work..." cried Lenny pointing at Gilly and Natalie.

Miss Dymock could immediately see that written work and pictures were now covered in scribbles from what looked suspiciously like marker pen.

"Did anyone see this happen?" she asked.

Lenny and Nathan cried out, "Yes, us."

Lenny tried to explain that when the other teacher left Natalie had brought out a packet of sweets from her pencil case and some wrapped biscuits from her cardigan pockets, and Gilly brought out a couple of bars of chocolate from her cardigan pockets, and they put them on the table where they were working and called out,

"Hey, let's have a feast while the teacher's not looking!"

Most of the curious children had left their work to go to have some sweets even though they looked suspiciously like the sweets which had gone missing from children's lunches. While most of the other children were engrossed, Natalie and Gilly slipped away from their table. Lenny and Nathan had hung back, undecided what to do, but too late and too far from their table to stop Gilly and Natalie from going to their table and scribbling on their work.

"You can't prove any of this, Miss," said Gilly and Natalie stepping forward to the front of the class looking quite aggressive. "I think it is really they are not any good at their work, so they scribbled over it themselves," said Natalie with Gilly adding, "Yeah, they are just dumb especially Nathan and Maisie... really dumb."

Suddenly, as if from nowhere the black cat with the yellow eyes appeared in the classroom. Mr Perkins leaped up onto the lectern and looked down at the two girls hissing.

"Please, Miss," said Gilly, "that thing is hissing at us."

With an athletic leap Mr Perkins was off the lectern and leaping first at Gilly and then at Natalie. Both cried with pain and pushed him away but in the melee some marker pens and several small jars fell out of their skirt pockets, two breaking at their feet, splattering red poster paint on their shoes and on their clothing. Mr Perkins leaped back onto the lectern looking down at the two cringing girls.

Tears began to roll down the cheeks of Gilly and Natalie.

"Get that thing away from us," they cried.

"Well," said Miss Dymock, "I think I have the evidence of who scribbled on the work and who broke into an art cupboard."

She instructed two uninvolved children to fetch Miss Deamer who appeared quite quickly. She looked at the scene and heard the accounts. Mr Perkins just sat tall on top of the lectern.

"Get that horrid cat away from me," cried Gilly. "And me too… he's dangerous," added Natalie.

"Well," said Miss Deamer, "he seems to have caught you red-handed or should I say red 'shoed' looking at the paint on you. Breaking into the art cupboard and then ruining someone's hard work is a very serious matter. He appears to have taught you both a valuable lesson, that if you keep doing bad things you will eventually get found out."

She paused and looked up at the cat who now sat there purring and just mouthed, "Thank you," silently. She did not say another word to the cat and escorted the two miscreants to the office.

That was the last time anyone saw Gilly and Natalie at that school. They were formally suspended. Their parents for their own reasons sent them both away to boarding school, where doubtless the two girls tried to be unpleasant to other children until they were found out.

Miss Dymock was left to make order out of chaos. She received multiple volunteers to clear up the mess. Mops and buckets were obtained and the helpful children soon cleared up the poster paint. She was unclear what Gilly and Natalie had intended to do with pots of poster paint but taking the pots had certainly backfired.

She addressed the class with the cat still perching on the top of the lectern looking both in charge of the class and inscrutable at the same time.

"Now, children, as some of you had their work damaged and one group has lost two members, I propose to give everyone an extra week to finish their projects."

She remembered to do a little signing for Maisie's benefit. Although Maisie could just about cope without British Sign Language, Miss Dymock found she did even better when someone could sign to her. She made a mental note to go on a refresher course.

Lenny, Nathan and Maisie all breathed a sigh of relief now the bullies had been taught a lesson and had left.

"I would so like to have a cat of my own," said Nathan.

Mr Perkins jumped down and rubbed himself around Nathan's legs and then around Miss Dymock's legs all the time purring.

"You are such a purry pussycat, a real Mr Perkins," she said. "I wonder if I should check if you are someone's cat."

Miss Dymock bent down as if to quickly pick him up, with thoughts of taking him to a vet or cat charity to see if he had a microchip, but he was too quick for her. He disappeared through the open classroom door with his tail held erect. When she peered out into the corridor he was gone.

Chapter 7

Mr Perkins to the Rescue

Lenny found the time passed rapidly. Half-term at school came and went. The children finished their projects and Aunt Lavinia came to the school again. She greeted the work with some enthusiasm. Lenny and Miss Deamer and Miss Dymock had told her what had happened. As she came into the classroom she said,

"I do hope I see that lovely black cat again."

Lenny and her parents went to have tea with Aunt Lavinia again. To Lenny's relief she had not made her terrible sandwiches this time. She said slightly apologetically,

"I have some little sausage rolls from the shop. I thought you might like something different."

She made a big fuss of Winnie who had been brought to the cottage at her request. She referred once again to missing her old dog Dickie but added,

"I think I will get another pet. I was even considering getting a cat. I was so impressed by that cat Mr Perkins. The only worry I have is traffic in the village."

Afternoon tea was a success and all smiles. On her tea table were books on cat care and leaflets on animal adoption. There were discussions about whether Aunt Lavinia could have a 'catio' ... part of her patio wired over to give a cat a safe outside space.

Tony mused that he wondered who owned Mr Perkins and from whence he came, but no-one had any answers. Mr Perkins came and went as he wished.

Bonfire Night soon arrived. Kate took Lenny to the school firework display while Tony stayed at home with Winnie. Some teachers assisted by a few parents put on a good display well away from the school buildings. Fortunately, Lenny's home was some distance away from any firework displays which might have disturbed Winnie. Lenny enjoyed seeing Nathan, Maisie and some of her other new friends. The children munched away on hot sausages and toffee apples. Lenny no longer thought so much about her old house and her old school.

As the glowing embers of the fire of the bonfire died down and the sky was no longer lit up by traces of rockets, the children and their parents began to make their way home. The night had become misty as it often did after Bonfire Night. Lenny could not be sure, but she thought she caught a glimpse of Mr Perkins' glowing eyes in the wood opposite her home. The thought of Mr Perkins passed from her mind as she was greeted by tail wags and licks from Winnie.

Brian and Tracey Wheeler managed to coax Sabrina to go with them to the pub Fireworks' Party. There was a small bonfire in the pub garden and Reg lit some Catherine wheels on an adjacent wall. They whirled around giving a brief but pretty display. The emphasis was more on traditional Bonfire Night food and drink. There was a general good-humoured atmosphere. There was a short pub quiz about Guy Fawkes and the origins of Bonfire Night. Although Reg was plainly very busy managing his staff and serving customers, he was delighted to see Sabrina and made a point of coming over to greet her.

"How is the dog walking progressing with Winnie?" he asked.

"She's a lovely dog," said Sabrina. "Although it is early days, I would say pretty well."

"I am so pleased Uncle Ron's dog went to a good home and that I sometimes get to see her," he replied.

"Uncle Ron?" queried Tracey who had been listening. Reg and Sabrina explained something of the dog's complicated history.

"I was still in the army when my uncle died so I couldn't take Winnie. It was so sad leaving her at the rescue kennels. They do such a good job I think I might do a fundraiser here at the pub. In due course it would also be nice for there to be a pub dog or a pub cat."

Sabrina and Tracey agreed with his ideas.

"Listen, I must get back to work, but…" he cleared his throat, "Sabrina, as you know Mondays are largely my day off. Please could I buy you a late lunch or an early afternoon tea at the farm shop this coming Monday since I would be very grateful if you could help me with the fundraiser."

"I would be very pleased to help," said Sabrina accepting the invitation.

Tracey did not comment as to why she was not asked as well since it was obvious Sabrina and Reg were developing a rapport and Reg seemed so different to Sabrina's terrible ex-husband from the descriptions her niece had given her. Brian indeed was socialising with Reg as well since the two men were going to approach the general and ask him if they couldn't organise a clay pigeon shoot on his land to raise money to improve facilities on the sports' field.

Christopher and Nathan were out very early morning with Deena at the stables. It was still dark but in the light from the lamps on the side of buildings they could see the steam from their own breath. They were all admiring a new occupant of the stables who was owned by a younger member of the general's family. 'Brilliant Breeze' was a spirited chestnut thoroughbred filly.

"Well," said Deena as Christopher and Nathan started to turn towards Christopher's car to make tracks to school and to work, "I have been thinking. Nathan, since you are making good progress, we might get a kitten if one becomes available. And if you continue to make good progress, I might organise some riding lessons for you in the New Year."

"Thank you, thank you, Mum," said Nathan.

As he sat in the car with Christopher he speculated about the colour of any possible kitten and the village mystery black cat came into the conversation.

"I like tortoiseshell cats and smoky grey ones. Or they could be black like Mr Perkins. Actually, I don't mind!" He paused. "I did wonder if Mr Perkins could be my cat, but no-one knows where he goes, and he just seems to turn up now and again."

"Yes," agreed Christopher, "it is a bit of a mystery. He seems to just turn up or so it seems, when he might be needed. But no-one has discovered his origins or how he manages it!"

"I think he is magic!" said Nathan.

Although Christopher had long since left beliefs of magic behind in childhood, he could not help himself responding, "Maybe he is."

Sometime later on a cold November Sunday morning the man Kenny was talking to a member of what might colloquially be called his gang.

"Right, Malc," he said to a muscular thickset bald man who may or may not have been called that name but who was certainly known by the gang as 'Big Malc', "I will make it worth your while to go to that village and try to confirm if that ex-wife of mine is living there. I don't want to be seen because when the time is ripe, I will go and get my revenge."

"It's well in the countryside, ain't it, boss?" said the man Malc scratching some tattoos on the side of his neck. "'Cos I also got something to get rid of…"

"You haven't gone and topped someone, 'ave you… cos I can't be doing with the fuzz doing searches for a body in that area," said Kenny half joking.

"Naw, boss," said Malc with an evil grin, "the missus got a cat which had kittens… I couldn't be doing with all that mewing, so I told her I would rehome them in a nice home in the countryside!"

He picked up a wriggling sack and added laconically, "Just cats."

"And there was I," said Kenny, "going to tell you not to let the cat out of the bag."

The two men laughed at what they thought was a joke. Then Malc placed the wriggling, mewing sack in a battered van and set off for Willowrose by Stow.

That Sunday afternoon Tony and Lenny had taken Winnie on a long country walk. They intended to call on Nathan's family at Twelve Tree Bottom. Attired in woolly hats, Wellington boots and heavy coats they soon developed a healthy glow as Winnie bounced enthusiastically down muddy paths. With the house to herself, Kate had free rein to do a little cleaning and to throw out accumulated rubbish before the bin men came on Monday. The bins sat on some stone flags close to the front gate but discreetly out of the way. As she approached the bins with a wastepaper basket in each hand, she heard a vehicle come clattering up the lane. A van which looked as if it had seen better days drew up by the woodland opposite.

A thickset man she did not recognise got out and pulled a sack out of a side door of the van. The sack seemed to be wriggling and there was a faint mewing sound. He dropped the sack into the undergrowth.

As Kate began to call out, "Hey, wait a minute," the man got back into the van and drove off at speed, tyres screeching.

As it happened Malc was initially unsuccessful in extracting any information from the locals. When he went into the pub and tried to ingratiate himself with the manager, this of course was Reg who was immediately suspicious of this most unattractive stranger who seemed very out of place. Reg would not be drawn on any local information whatsoever and so Malc did not want to raise further suspicion by mentioning Sabrina by name or that he was looking for a specific person. He made vague coarse jokes about whether there were any divorced women in the village who might need a bit of company. He had no luck in the farm shop either, who if anything were less connected with the community than the pub. The café waitress just shook her head and looked confused when he asked if there were any divorced women looking for company.

Big Malc parked his van near the edge of the village just on the corner of the new estate and he was looking on his phone at a photo of Sabrina which

Kenny had provided and was thinking about what to do next. He really didn't want to disappoint the boss. He took a cigarette from his pocket and held his lighter up. He looked up ready to light his cigarette. There were some clattering noises from within the estate. A few of the householders had put their bins out ready for the dustmen on Monday morning. Not far down the road he saw an attractive woman was wheeling out a bin to the kerb. It was the girl in the photograph on his phone. Kenny would be pleased. Malc could identify the road and through the large white number painted on the bin, even the house number. He smiled and put his cigarette and lighter away again and drove away to bring Kenny the information he craved.

Kate had been left wondering what to do. She was sure there was something alive in the sack, and indeed it might be something which needed rescuing, but on the other hand she was fearful someone might for example have thrown away an unwanted pet poisonous snake. She put down the empty wastepaper bins and she peered across the road undecided as to what to do next.

Suddenly Mr Perkins appeared from the wood with a loud, "Miaow." He stood for a few seconds on the verge and then he dashed into the undergrowth and about a minute later re-appeared carrying a smoky grey kitten by the scruff of the neck. He crossed the road and dropped the kitten gently at Kate's feet. Then he went back across the road and after another minute returned with a ginger and white kitten. For a third time Mr Perkins brought a kitten from across the road and placed it at Kate's feet, this time a grey and ginger kitten, with the odd white patch. Then he disappeared again. This time he was quite some time. Kate placed the kittens in one of the empty bins and was again undecided what to do next. She was about to take the kittens to the house when there was a loud, "Miaow," from Mr Perkins. He seemed to be looking at her from under the bracken.

He said, "Miaow," again and stared at her with his yellow eyes. She felt she was being summonsed. She put the three kittens in the bin in a safe position in the front garden and cautiously followed Mr Perkins across the road. His tail was erect, and he kept looking at her to follow him. She struggled a short way into the bracken and brambles. There was the sack in front of her and beside it was a beautiful tortoiseshell kitten. Half in and half out of the sack was a tortoiseshell cat who she presumed was the mother of the kittens. There did not appear to be any further kittens. The mother was making a pathetic mewing noise. Kate gingerly approached the sack and bent down to see if she could extract the mother, who had one of her claws caught in the sack.

At first the mother cat hissed and put out a front paw as if to scratch her.

"Miaow," said Mr Perkins and rubbed himself around Kate's legs as if to demonstrate she was a friend.

"It's all right, beautiful girl," said Kate in soft tones. She gently pulled the sack off from around the cat's haunches and shook the sack to loosen it from round the claw. There did not seem to be anything else in the sack, so she quickly scooped up the now freed tortoiseshell mother in her arms, all the time making gentle reassuring comments. Mr Perkins picked up the kitten by the scruff of the neck and they proceeded back across the lane.

Quickly, she took the mother cat to the enclosed back porch, Winnie's former abode but until now free of other animals. Mr Perkins followed and deposited the kitten with her mother. She grabbed some old towels from a shelf and put them down on the ground and having put the door to, she quickly went outside and grabbed the bin of three kittens. She fetched a small bowl of water and tried to make mother and kitties as comfortable as she could. She slipped into the kitchen which was free of Winnie since she was on her walk and improvised on food for the mother. She quickly tore up a slice of cold chicken on a saucer and presented it to the hungry mother cat who ate ravenously. As she sought to secure the outer door she looked out for Mr Perkins, but he was gone. She felt regretful she could not give Mr Perkins some chicken too but concentrated on making mum and kitties as comfortable as possible. The inner door was closed, and she decided that for now the outer door of the porch should be closed, for the safety of the tiny kittens.

She waited at the front of the house for Tony, Lenny and Winnie to return. It was getting dark when they came bounding down the lane. She met them at the gate. Tony could tell Kate was concerned about something.

"Whatever you do," she said, "do not let Winnie into the back porch."

"What's gone wrong now?" said Tony with a look of concern.

"Nothing," said Kate, "but there is a mother cat and four kittens in there... and in fact, Tony, I urgently need you to go to the shop and buy cat food."

"How on earth? What on earth?" Tony stumbled for the right words.

Kate quickly explained about the van and the sack, and the rescue in effect made by Mr Perkins. Tony found himself being chivvied to get in his car and head for the shop before it closed. Twenty minutes later he was back with a box of wet cat food, a box of kitten food and a box of dry cat food. He also had a bag of cat litter.

He found Kate and Lenny were crouching down in the porch looking at the mother suckling her assorted kittens. He could not help but admire the scene himself.

"I think I'll get a seed tray from the garden to make a cat litter tray until we can get to a pet store... and we need to give them a nice warm blanket."

"Shhhh," said Kate and Lenny together, but afterwards they praised and thanked Tony for his purchases and for the seed tray idea.

"That cat Mr Perkins seems to have a knack for being at the right place at the right time," said Tony.

Kate and Lenny agreed with him, and then discussion turned to naming the cats.

"I think the mummy should be called Bella," said Lenny. "I heard on TV it means beautiful."

"Goodness, you are right!" said Kate. "OK."

"How about Carmen for the tortoiseshell kitten?" suggested Tony. "That's a Spanish name to go with Bella."

"Sure," said Kate and Lenny smiled in agreement.

Lenny said, "The grey one should be called Smokey, the ginger and white one Marmalade, and grey and ginger one should be called... I don't know!"

They laughed and Kate said, "What about Bastet after the Egyptian cat god?"

Tony raised his eyebrows and Lenny misunderstood and said,

"Basket is an awful name! What about… what about Brandy?"

Tony and Kate didn't correct her about misunderstanding the name of the Egyptian god. They did not want to spoil the moment. Bella, Carmen, Smokey, Marmalade and Brandy were for now content in the old back porch. The kittens suckled their mother who was purring with contentment. Then Tony, Kate and Lenny sat down in the living room and enjoyed steaming mugs of hot chocolate with Winnie lying by the hearth eating a dog chew. Outside it was dark and misty. Lenny thought she saw the glint of some yellow eyes peering through the window, but then the image was gone. All for now seemed right with the world.

Chapter 8

Of Kittens, Cats and Corgis

Kenny was not as pleased as Big Malc would have hoped.

"You will have to go back, find out more about her habits. I want to try and get her when she is alone."

Big Malc sighed. It had not been easy the first time he visited Willowrose.

"Okay, okay," said Kenny sensing the other man's reluctance, "leave it for now. I will have a look online… see if I spot anything about her or her family in social media."

He now turned his attention to the operation with which he was currently involved, namely smuggling drugs into the country disguised within shipments of tractor parts. He would get this done and then he would take his revenge. After all, revenge would be that much sweeter if he took his time over it.

The object of his desire for revenge, Sabrina was in complete ignorance of the continued danger. She had been having a good few days. Dog walking with Winnie was going well. The training at school to be a lunchtime supervisor was complete and now she was taking tentative steps to train to be a classroom assistant. Her friendship with Reg continued. He did not press her to move too fast with dating. They had been out for their cycle rides and coffees. They had been to the cinema in the complex near the motorway junction and had eaten burgers afterwards. She had eaten a quick lunch or two with him in the private quarters of the pub. She was happy with the way things were progressing.

Reg seemed content as well. If he had any complaints, he certainly didn't say anything. His main complaint at the moment was how he was going to sort out having a pub cat or dog since he felt this would make the place more homely. He also had some niggles about sorting out the charity clay pigeon shoot, due to the nature of General Bluffington. He felt the general was making matters unnecessarily complex. Last time he had spoken to Brian Wheeler and the general, the old boy had unrolled a big chart on a table in the pub which was intended to show the layout of the event, to include everything from temporary toilets and parking to ammunition storage. It looked like a series of scribbles to Reg. Nonetheless, the general had taken a pencil from his pocket and started to point to various areas on his plan.

"Participants will enter here and here," in ringing tones.

"Toilets are here, here and here," he continued.

Reg tried to dismiss thoughts of the general from his mind by thinking about Sabrina and cats.

Adrianne Deamer and Cecilia Dymock found their recent discussions had turned to keeping pets.

"I keep thinking about how nice it would be to have a dog," said Miss Deamer to Miss Dymock as they got ready to walk down to the school.

"I blame that cat who hangs around here," answered Miss Dymock.

As if he had been called Mr Perkins appeared just outside their front door.

"Miaow," he said loudly and knocked over an umbrella stand in the porch. The umbrellas came clattering out together with a clutch of dusty leaflets which had somehow ended up in there. Adrianne Deamer bent down with a sigh and picked up the leaflets. Most of them were adverts for a local freezer store although a couple were about dog rescue. One leaflet caught her eye. It had a picture of a corgi on the front of it, and it was headed 'Derek and David's Dachshund and Corgi Rescues'. A further leaflet for the dog rescue kennels which had accommodated Winnie, and which had floated down in front of her feet was put to one side.

"Look at this," she said to Cecilia Dymock, "they only appear to be about thirty miles away… I wonder."

Cecilia Dymock smiled. "It's that cat again!" She turned to look at Mr Perkins, but he had gone.

After the end of the school day the two women went online and learned more about the small rescue kennels. It appeared there were not many animals for re-homing, but a three-year-old corgi caught their attention. The ad said 'Bobo… Three years old, needing a new home after his owner was evicted. House trained but nervous. This friendly soul is good to be adopted as soon as possible'.

They resolved to contact the kennels and so it was Adrianne found herself talking to Derek on the phone the next day. To her surprise he seemed quite suspicious of her.

"We can't have just anyone adopting one of our dogs. David and I are very particular. We shall have to fully vet you."

"How is that done?" Adrienne queried, thinking she would like to go to the kennels.

"Well before you even meet one of our babies David and I will have to come and inspect your premises. Then we will collect the adoption fee of £500."

She found herself making arrangements for Derek and David to come round for coffee and an inspection the very next Saturday. She sat with Cecilia Dymock for a bit and made a list of all the things they needed for the adoption, from food through to suitable bedding. Then she started to order items online and with a smile said,

"This is so exciting!"

When Saturday arrived the two women had a tray ready for tea or coffee, they had a dog bed and some basic dog food. Even though it was winter a sports car with its top down arrived. It was a bit of a surprise to Miss Deamer and Miss Dymock to see this silver gleaming affair and two men in it dressed in what looked like vintage flying jackets emerge. They invited them indoors.

Derek turned out to be tall, thin and blond, dressed in an elegant pale grey suit. David on the other hand was short, swarthy and sported a handle-bar moustache and a vintage tweed suit incorporating baggy knicker-bockers. They were given a tour of the bungalow and its enclosed sheltered garden.

Adrianne Deamer politely asked,

"Tea or coffee?"

Derek replied, "That would be lovely if you have hibiscus?"

"Sorry, English breakfast or camomile," she said.

The reply was, "Camomile will have to do I suppose."

Cecilia Dymock asked,

"I take it the dog is fully vaccinated?"

Derek and David looked at each other guiltily. "Eh," said David, "we thought so, but someone forgot there was no vaccination card. So, it will mean starting from scratch, but if you are keen you won't mind that will you?"

Cecilia Dymock asked, "He is good-natured I understand?"

"He can snap a little at first," said Derek vaguely.

Adrianne Deamer started to probe further, "The ad says he is housetrained but nervous. Is he fully housetrained?"

"Well," said David, "he is when he is not in a nervous state, so we understand... he does not like the sound of fireworks, other dogs barking, loud people's laughter or shouting, singing, thunder, heavy rain..."

"So, he is not really housetrained, is he?" Adrianne probed further.

"No," was the response.

Cecilia Dymock asked, "Do you think he could be taught? Could a behaviourist help his nerves?"

Both men went a bit pink and were reluctant to respond or to give any further information. David cleared his throat and said,

"Would you like to pay the adoption fee now? I can give you details so you can do a bank transfer."

Adrianne Deamer and Cecilia Dymock looked at each other. As a chorus they said,

"No."

Then Adrianne politely showed their guests to the door and said,

"I don't think we will be proceeding but thank you for coming."

As the men drove down the driveway, she noticed a black shape on an old bit of dry stone wall quite a way from the bungalows but just in view. She was not certain but thought it was the cat who was often around. He seemed to jump down away from the drive and send pieces of loose stone flying everywhere. One hit the bonnet of the sports car with a clunk. The car stopped briefly. There was a bit of swearing about 'damaged paint' and then the men were gone.

Miss Deamer was not sorry; she then slumped down on the settee. The two women sat despondently together speculating on David and Derek's motives. It was quite unclear if the issues which arose were as a result of bad intent to get £500 and get the dog off their hands or whether it was just carelessness. But they resolved to keep looking for another dog or dogs. They got out the other crumpled dog rescue leaflet and put it on the coffee table.

Lenny on the other hand was far from despondent as she sat playing with the kittens. Within days they were eating the kitten food which Tony had thoughtfully purchased, and it was clear the kittens would soon be ready for new homes. Smokey had already been reserved for Nathan. He had seriously informed Lenny and his parents that if it was at all possible, he wanted to train Smokey to be a therapy cat. Christopher said,

"You never cease to amaze me, where did you get that idea?"

"On social media," he replied. "In America there are one or two well-known trained cats who go into old folks' homes, even hospitals... and the old people love to stroke the cats, and it makes them so happy to hear them purring and sometimes they remember a pet they used to have. I would like to get my cat to be a cat like that."

Christopher reflected that many cats would be far from therapeutic, bringing in dead rodents or birds, but he supposed the purring sound of a cat was a very calming sound. It did seem a nice idea. He wondered if Smokey could be trained or not. If that was what Nathan wanted to do, within reason he would support him with such a worthy proposal. In the meantime, he encouraged Nathan to make a list of what Smokey needed so they could go to a pet store together. He was delighted by the positive improvements which Nathan had shown recently.

On the next school day Nathan chatted to Lenny about his interest in therapy cats and his plans to see if Smokey might be trained to be a therapy cat. The two children were engrossed in conversation when Kate drew up to collect Lenny. She had been busy in the Family Court, so she was pleased she had not had to leave Lenny to find her way to Aunt Lavinia's cottage, which was her emergency strategy when she was delayed, or when Lenny could not go home with Nathan.

As it happened Sabrina had been walking Winnie and came up to chat to Kate. The two women had quite a rapport and when Sabrina heard that Kate represented people in Family Court, she mentioned she had suffered a bad marriage, and she realised how strenuous things must be for Kate with all manner of different clients to accompany to court. Soon Nathan's mother appeared so Lenny waved goodbye to him and got in the car.

"Sabrina, do you want to pop Winnie in the back and hop in yourself rather than walk to our house?" asked Kate. "We could have a natter over a cuppa."

Sabrina readily agreed and soon she was enjoying a cup of tea with Kate, while Lenny inspected the kittens before starting her homework which she tended to do before having an early dinner with her parents (except if Tony was stuck at work). Sabrina little by little opened up about her past and also mentioned that she was seeing Reg the pub manager.

"He seems very different to men who I have known in the past," she said, "he has even mentioned he wants to get a cat."

Kate said, "Perhaps he might like a kitten," and she took Sabrina to see the kittens. Sabrina asked how Kate ended up with the cat and kittens. Kate told her the story of Mr Perkins in effect rescuing them. And so it was Sabrina found herself telling the story to Reg next time she saw him.

"That black cat sounds very intriguing," he said. "Pity he is so elusive!"

Nonetheless, despite his fascination with Mr Perkins he found himself going to see the kittens with Sabrina.

"Well, I have to have Brandy," he said. "What a good name for a pub cat!"

Kate agreed but also mentioned that next day she was taking all the cats to the vet to be microchipped and for health checks.

"Don't worry," said Reg, "I will have him when he is ready but meanwhile I am happy to make a contribution to his upkeep."

"That is very kind, but you don't have to do so," said Kate.

Reg then spoke out loud his thoughts of providing for Brandy; of having a cat door at the rear of the pub where the dustbin area had a high fence and discouraging Brandy from going to the car park by giving him this rear exit. He talked of putting a cat bed by the fireplace. Despite his military background Kate gained the impression that Reg was actually a gentle, thoughtful soul and he might be just the man for Sabrina. Sabrina seemed much more confident and content these days. Indeed, when she was next walking Winnie near the school, she found it was Adrianne Deamer who came rushing out and asked her advice.

"I believe Lenny's mother got Winnie from the dog rescue?" she mentioned the name.

"Yes," said Sabrina.

"I wondered if they seemed OK," she queried. "Cecilia and I have had a strange and disappointing experience."

"Kate seems very happy with how things went with Winnie," said Sabrina. "Why?"

Miss Deamer related the strange experience with Derek and David.

"I have no idea if they were conmen or just odd," she said, "but we still want a dog. In fact, if anything the bad experience has made us even more determined."

"I should go online and see if there is any dog you fancy and then make an appointment to go to the kennels," advised Sabrina, initially shivering a little at the word 'conmen'. Then she dismissed her instinctive fears.

"If I get a moment," was the response. "Would you believe Christmas festivities will soon be on us as we are into November, and I must remind Cecilia to start carol service rehearsals."

Just as Sabrina was advising Adrianne Deamer about the dog rescue, Tony Tadworth found himself receiving a telephone call from Aunt Lavinia.

"I need legal advice, and I need it now… so come on your way home from work."

She seemed very agitated and quite distressed, so he thought he better do as she required.

"Sit," she said as he came in her cottage, and he found himself being presented with a weak, greyish cup of tea.

"You are an experienced solicitor," she said.

"Yes, these days I am a partner," said Tony wondering what was coming next.

"Well," said Aunt Lavinia, "not having my Dickie has made me realise I may not be around much longer myself. My will is not up to date. It really has been worrying me. I lay awake all last night worrying about what might happen if I died."

Tony began to realise it was not really an emergency, except in Aunt Lavinia's mind. The old lady was probably made of cast iron, but he sat and listened to her concerns.

"You see I would like money to put aside for Leonora to go to university and I don't want the taxman to get my estate. There is this cottage, and I have investments as well. My old will left my estate to dead people."

Tony smiled. "First, there are allowances on estates so generally it is bigger estates which bear the brunt of inheritance tax. As we are family, and Lenny is my daughter I don't think I should draw up your will myself. In my mind it might be a conflict of interest if I advise you, although the reality is we are on the same page. I will pass the details of your wishes to one of our wills and probate people and tell them to advise you as soon as possible… Don't worry about there being a bill from the firm, I will settle it."

"Thank you," she said and tried to pass him a stale looking biscuit.

She then smiled weakly. "But what if I get dementia in the future? I have been worrying about that as well. Who will look after my affairs?"

Tony replied, "You can have a document drawn up called a Lasting Power of Attorney appointing someone to look after your affairs in that hopefully unlikely scenario. The wills and probate department can help you with that as well."

"I think I would appoint you and Kate," she said.

Then Aunt Lavinia smiled at Tony. "You are making me feel much better. When the cottage feels empty at night, I lie awake and worry about things."

"Why don't you come and have tea with the family very soon. You can see the new kittens." Aunt Lavinia was already aware of the rescue of the mother cat and kittens.

"That would be lovely."

Tony felt he should encourage Aunt Lavinia to have a kitten.

"You know a pussycat would be good company for you," added Tony. "We could have a catio added to the back of the cottage so the kitty would not get into the traffic in the village."

"A catio?" asked Aunt Lavinia, apparently not recalling a previous discussion. "That sounds intriguing."

"It is simply a wired in safe space for a cat or cats, often in a patio area so that a cat can go outside without being able to wander off into danger," replied Tony patiently.

"I like the sound of that, and I would love to come to tea. I am not committing myself to anything, but I will look at the kittens."

Tony hoped that tonight she might dream of kittens rather than lie awake worrying about her will. He was soon putting on his coat and heading out into the dark night air. A black shape was sitting on the garden wall with glowing yellow eyes.

"Have you got something to do with this?" he said.

As his breath came out as steam in the freezing air Mr Perkins was gone again and Tony wondered if he had ever been there at all.

Chapter 9

New Homes for Christmas

When Aunt Lavinia came to tea at Lenny's house, Kate and Tony rolled out the proverbial red carpet. Kate made little smoked salmon sandwiches and served miniature quiches and sausage rolls. She obtained a mouthwatering chocolate Yule log, and some individual Christmas cake slices from The Impossible Pig Farm Shop and hoped Aunt Lavinia did not expect 'home-made' fair. Tony fetched Aunt Lavinia in his car and Lenny and Winnie were under strict instructions to be well behaved.

As it happened Aunt Lavinia loved Winnie and was entranced with the cat and kittens. A chair was drawn up for her and she would have gladly spent all afternoon fussing and stroking Bella and playing with the kittens.

"Do you think I could have a mother and child?" she asked. "Maybe Bella and Carmen…I love their tortoiseshell coats, and I would have the time to give them attention."

At first Lenny looked a bit crestfallen but Kate came to the rescue,

"What a good idea," she said, "Smokey will go to Nathan, Brandy will go to Reg at the pub, Bella and Carmen will go to Aunt Lavinia and Marmalade will be Lenny's new best friend here. And we can all go and visit the various cats too as they will be local!"

Lenny soon cheered up when she realised Marmalade would be staying. A cheerful afternoon tea followed. Tony promised he would do his best to find someone to build the catio for Aunt Lavinia in time for Christmas. And so, on an evening soon after he found himself chatting to Brian Wheeler and Reg in the pub.

"Don't you worry," said Brian, "if need be, I will do it myself. It's a great idea for the cats and for the old lady. I wish I could do something to cheer up the old general, rattling around in that huge hall. His wife died years ago, and his son is busy with the army. I think the son's family follow him around with his postings."

Reg said, "I don't get a lot of time, but I might be able to give you a hand. I have just about finished tweaking the little backyard so that Brandy can go out there. I am looking forward to having him very soon."

Tony couldn't help but notice that Christopher was also in the pub. He was closeted away in the corner with the general and Tony gesticulated to Brian to lower his tone but fortunately it didn't seem that the general had heard him, let alone knew he was there. After a few minutes Christopher waved to Tony to join them. As Tony sat down Christopher said,

"The general is considering transferring all his personal business and that of the estate to our firm, since he is impressed with our work sorting out the trust."

"Jolly good show from you fellows," he said.

"I seem to have made a bit of a mess of the estate deeds and also future inheritance tax planning, so I hope you can help me get things straight... maybe I should have a good luck charm like that cat, don't you know!"

"I am sure we can help you with your deeds and inheritance tax planning," said Tony, although he didn't see the general as the right person to have a cat so he was silent on the subject.

"Mind you," continued the general, "a dog might be better... I used to have a good gun dog Bessie." He went on at some length about Bessie's virtues. These days Brian Wheeler's assistant provided his three gun dogs as and when required if there was the occasional shoot at the estate.

"We adopted a dog from the dog rescue place," said Tony rapidly thinking matters out as he spoke. "What might work well for you would be to sponsor a long-term doggy resident in the kennels. Then you might be able to visit the dog without the burden of looking after him or her in your home."

"What a great idea," said Christopher cottoning on to Tony's train of thought. "I am sure they would appreciate it with Christmas coming up."

"Splendid! Splendid!" said the general. "I rattle around all on my own in the Hall so it would be nice to visit the doggies."

Other people considering the dog rescue kennels were Adrianne Deamer and Cecilia Dymock. They sat side by side looking at the computer screen, reading details of the dogs needing homes. Each had an appealing picture but some of the descriptions left concerns from 'no recall' to 'cannot associate with other dogs'. There were no dogs who remotely looked like corgis. Eventually they reached a picture of the last two dogs on the list. The photograph showed them sitting together and the description read as follows:

'Rufus and Scruff

Rufus and Scruff are best pals, and we would like to rehome them together. Currently they are with a foster carer. They were rescued from a household with multiple pets all of whom had been neglected. Rufus appears to be a Red Setter spaniel cross and Scruff a Staffie lurcher cross. Both medium sized dogs are housetrained and are fully vaccinated. We believe Rufus is about 4 years old and Scruff is about 5-6 years old. While they have not presented concerns with children they would benefit from a quiet household where they are the only pets. Both dogs like playing ball and enjoy tummy rubs.'

Adrianne found herself staring at their picture. She thought about playing ball with them in the back garden. Her thoughts were interrupted by Cecilia Dymock speaking,

"I like them," she said. "Do you reckon we should make an appointment?"

"Absolutely," was the reply.

And so, on Saturday morning the two women found themselves at the rescue kennels which had rescued Winnie. A flustered young woman greeted them.

"I am the assistant manager, June. I am so sorry we haven't got the boys out of the kennels in readiness for you, but we have had an interruption. My manager is sorting the matter out."

They could just about hear the strident tones of General Bluffington. He had liked the sponsorship suggestion so much he had taken it upon himself to turn up at the kennels without an appointment, and the kennels being always in need of funds did not want to turn him away.

"I thought I might organise a fundraising sale at the hall," he said, "although I might sponsor the odd dog if that suited you."

June took Miss Deamer and Miss Dymock to Rufus and Scruff's kennel.

"You can walk them on our exercise field if you wish," said June.

"That would be lovely," was the reply and indeed walkies were enjoyed around the field with each dog looking at the women with a longing gaze which seemed to say, 'Take me home, take me home'. Strokes and tummy tickles were in order at the end of the walk together with a few dog treats.

"Right," said Miss Deamer, "what do we do next to adopt them?"

"We would like to bring them home for Christmas," added Miss Dymock.

June went through the necessary forms with them and arranged an urgent home inspection which she said she believed would be a formality. Both women went to the dogs' kennel before they left and said, "Home soon, home soon," in chorus.

Nearby they could hear the general. He had been brought to the kennels of the two oldest residents, Humphrey a thirteen-year-old labrador and Elsie a ten-year-old bulldog who had health issues.

"These two are far too set in their ways to successfully rehome," said the manager, "what with special diets and medication and them being a bit grumpy."

"Sounds like me!" said the general with a laugh. A chair was brought for him, and the manager left him sitting there, making one sided small talk to the dogs who looked a bit puzzled. After about an hour the manager went to check if he was alright and found him sound asleep as were the dogs.

"I will come back on Christmas Eve with dog treats and dog toys," he said after he had fully awoken. "If you tell me what these two are allowed, I will bring them something special."

The general was looking forward to coming on Christmas Eve. He had not told anyone but there was doubt whether his son would come home at Christmas, such was the nature of his son's posting. Now he had somewhere positive he needed to be, and it gave him pleasure to go shopping for doggy Christmas presents.

Aunt Lavinia was also excited. The catio was due to be finished in the run-up to Christmas and then Bella and Carmen would move to her house. There would be a cat door leading out from her back door to the catio. She had their beds in place although she was sure she wouldn't mind if they sat on the end of her bed as Dickie had done. She hoped the pussycats would forgive her when she spent Christmas Day with Tony, Kate and Lenny.

Smokey had already gone to live with Nathan (and Brandy was moving the day after tomorrow). Lenny was a little sorry but on the other hand she was pleased that Nathan now had his own cat. Although Lenny exchanged a few messages with old friends she no longer missed her old house or her old school. She very much looked forward to Christmas. She thoroughly enjoyed making home-made cards in art class and rehearsing for the carol service. It was great to have Winnie and Marmalade and her friends locally such as Nathan. Sometimes she thought she saw the black cat with the yellow eyes out of the window and hoped that Mr Perkins was happy too.

Sabrina also glanced at Mr Perkins when she was walking Winnie and momentarily wondered what he was doing. She was so much more content and settled these days. She felt secure enough to agree to help with a New Year's Eve firework display on the field. Her name was mentioned on the Trust Facebook page as an organiser although Tracey's name was given as the principal contact for tickets. When Tracey had a phone call from a man enquiring about arrangements, and claiming to be from the local council, Tracey had no suspicions about the call.

"Who will be checking the venue and making sure it is secure after the event?" the man asked Tracey.

"That will be my niece Sabrina Wheeler," was the response, "she is a key holder at the school, and we will be borrowing their facilities to provide hot drinks and snacks and give people access to the toilets."

"Thank you, that is most helpful," said the man. "And what time will the event finish?"

"About 12.30," said Tracey.

"I expect you will be helping your niece," said the man.

"My husband and I will be marshalling people outside on the field. Sabrina will be okay on her own," she responded.

"Thank you so much," the man said.

Kenny was now sure he would have a good Christmas. He would look forward to New Year's when he felt he could now deal with Sabrina and get his revenge. He chuckled as he looked at a handgun on his desk in front of him. Oh, yes, it sounded as if he could get in and out before anyone realised, he was there. He also felt sure others would still be letting off fireworks nearby which would hopefully mask the noise of a shot.

Reg was totally unaware of the danger facing Sabrina. He had his plans which he hoped Sabrina would like. It was his intention to move Brandy into the pub in a few days' time. He invited Sabrina to take supper with him in the flat on the first evening for Brandy at his new home. He had also invited Brian, Tracey and Sabrina to have Christmas dinner at the pub. Although there would be some paying guests, he intended that he should enjoy the festivities as well. Reg had also managed to sneak away for a shopping trip in the big city.

He found his way first into a department store where he bought a tweed jerkin for Brian and a large basket of perfumes and fancy bath oils for Tracey. He stood for a long time outside the neighbouring store which was an upmarket jewellery store. He knew what he would like his future to be with Sabrina, but he was unsure if she was ready. Then his gaze rested on some pendants. On the end of silver chains were little silver dogs encrusted with dark semi-precious stones. He knew he had at least to buy her a dog pendant for Christmas.

Once inside the store he could not help but be drawn to the engagement rings. He looked for quite a while until he spotted a ring with a black onyx stone which somehow reminded him of that black cat which hung around the village. The setting was in the shape of a cat's head. He decided to be bold and buy it as well as the pendant. He hoped he might be able to offer it to Sabrina.

Christmas at Willowrose proved to be a genuinely joyful time. School term had ended well with a carol service with happy enthusiastic children. Smokey had settled well with Nathan and Brandy was settling down to be the pub cat. A sparkle could be found in Aunt Lavinia's eyes since Bella and Carmen had moved into her cottage. They had certainly fallen on all four paws since Aunt Lavinia was lavishing tuna and chicken breast on them.

On Christmas Day Lenny kept telling her parents and Aunt Lavinia that it was the best Christmas she had ever had. She enjoyed presents from her parents, but she also enjoyed giving treats to Winnie and Marmalade. Kate had taken her on a special trip to a pet shop so she could spend her pocket money on the right sort of treat. She gave each of her parents and Aunt Lavinia home-made cards which she had made at school, together with little felt bookmarks and pincushions which she had also made at school. The gifts were well received. Aunt Lavinia even gave her an unexpectedly nice gift. It was a little metal money box with pictures of dogs and cats on it. It seemed to be of some age.

"It was given to me when I was about your age," said Aunt Lavinia, "so it is only right you should have it now. I have put a few coins in it for luck!"

Lenny went and hugged Aunt Lavinia and to everyone's surprise she was quite receptive to the embrace and hugged Lenny back.

Adrianne Deamer and Cecilia Dymock sat down to roast chicken on Christmas Day. Sitting quietly by their dining room table were Rufus and Scruff who sat looking at them with adoring eyes. The two women had decided they would not feed the dogs titbits from the table, but both dogs had become well aware that if they were patient, they would get a large bowl each of tasty scraps. Once everyone had eaten their fill it was coats on for a bracing country walk. The day ended with contented snoozes from animals and humans by the fire.

The general was also having a good day. The recent clay pigeon shoot had been a success, and he had very much enjoyed his Christmas Eve afternoon with his new doggy companions at the kennels. Although there was a Boxing Day shoot on the estate, he resolved he would make time to return to the kennels before New Year's Eve. He saw the logic of not having to care for a dog himself in the hall but being able to visit dogs. On Christmas Day morning he had a long video call with his son who promised to visit him on the second weekend in January which cheered him immensely. As he strolled from his car into the pub for his Christmas lunch carrying a heavy looking carrier bag, he noticed Mr Perkins sitting on a wall. It was almost as if the cat was winking at him.

"You crafty devil," he said, "you are always up to something."

The cat looked enigmatic.

Inside the pub, there was much jollity. Hot punch was being served as people arrived. Most of the pub was given over to tables booked for Christmas dinner, although the snug near the back had been left for those wanting a quiet Christmas drink. The pub was open from noon until 9pm which more than satisfied those wanting to celebrate Christmas at the pub. Brandy who was growing fast from a kitten to a young cat had a basket on the counter of the lounge bar and a small dish of cat treats beside him. He seemed amazingly unfazed by the loud voices and laughter.

There was a roaring fire in both the grate of the lounge bar and the grate of the saloon bar. Although they had already been decorated with the ubiquitous tinsel Reg and Sabrina had been out on Christmas Eve and had gathered sprigs of holly which now adorned the beams. Reg had put the general on the table where Brian, Tracey, himself and Sabrina would be dining rather than letting the old fellow sit on his own. Presents were exchanged. Sabrina glowed pink and gave a beaming smile when she received her pendant. Reg found himself presented with a tweed cap and a silver hip flask by Sabrina.

To Reg's surprise the general produced gifts from his bag with a flourish, bottles of fine Scotch whisky for Brian and himself, and fine Chablis for Sabrina and Tracey. Finally, he produced a huge bottle, a jeroboam of Burgundy which he placed on the bar near the surprised kitten. Reg wondered how he had managed to carry the enormous bottle indoors.

The general staggered to his feet and pointed to the bottle,

"To everyone here who knows me, have a glass of wine on me. This has been an excellent Christmas Day… one of the best I have known. Cheers and season's greetings!"

Chapter 10

Someone learns a lesson

The men of the Police Tactical Firearms Unit were not pleased to be put on notice that they were on an Operation on New Year's Eve. As it happened the police had been watching Kenny for some time and were biding their time before they raided his warehouse. As it also happened what Kenny had no way of knowing was that Big Malc had served him up on a platter to the police.

Big Malc had drunk one too many on Boxing Day night and had managed to crash his van into a lamppost early the next morning. He was uninjured. His van was in a very bad way. Not only did the police show up and breathalyse him, but they also spotted a pack of drugs on the front seat which he was supposed to deliver for Kenny sometime in the near future. Big Malc was arrested. A deal was struck. In order that Big Malc would not have the book thrown at him, he readily gave up all he knew about Kenny including the drug smuggling and the fact that he believed Kenny was going to shoot his ex-wife at the turn of the New Year. He was even able to suggest it might be at Willowrose by Stow. Kenny hadn't particularly noticed his absence; he assumed Big Malc was somewhere celebrating. He was also much engrossed in his private thoughts of revenge.

The police decided that their Tactical Firearms Unit had better discreetly follow Kenny wherever he went on New Year's Eve. Another police team would raid his warehouse.

Knowing none of this Sabrina was taking a full part in the Firework Extravaganza on the sports' field. Most of the village were there although many had left radios and televisions playing music so as to help their animals. Lenny's family considered their home was far enough from the village not to be affected by the noise of fireworks but still left Mozart and Brahms playing in case Winnie and Marmalade needed distraction. Nathan and his family believed their home and the stables were too far to be affected by the fireworks at all. So, Lenny and Nathan stifled yawns, drank hot chocolate and saw the New Year's Eve fireworks on the field. Then they went home to be tucked into their beds. In Lenny's case, Winnie and Marmalade snuggled up on the end of her bed as if they had always belonged there.

Aunt Lavinia felt she was too old for fireworks but cuddled up with Bella and Carmen in front of her warm fire, feeling very content. The cats purred with contentment. From being abandoned in a sack they now had everything they could want, from tuna to cat treats, from cushions by the fire to small trees for climbing in the catio.

Cecilia Dymock was tasked with making sure the dogs were not frightened so she stayed at home with them playing her favourite recordings of the ethnic music of South Asia and offering them treats, while Adrianne Deamer attended the display. Adrianne looked forward to having a belated New Year drink on her return and to New Year's Day walkies. Somehow their household now felt complete.

Reg spent most of his evening managing the pub, with Brandy shut in the flat upstairs with music playing. The general could be seen popping backwards and forwards between the field and the lounge bar. The general purchased a bottle of brandy which he proceeded to take to the field for topping up some of the adults' hot chocolates! Reg had arranged with Sabrina to come to the pub after she had finished locking up the school. There was something special he wanted to discuss with Sabrina.

Unbeknownst to the residents of Willowrose as they cheered in the New Year at midnight and sang Auld Lang Syne, Kenny was drawing into a layby less than a mile from the village. He lit a cigarette and thought about what he was going to do with quiet satisfaction. He lit a second cigarette and then cursed as he had let his car fill with smoke, so he opened the car window fully. He put the cigarette out and got his pistol out which he loaded with a number of bullets. He held up the gun and made as if to aim it, taking the safety catch off, intending that this just be for a second for practice.

Kenny was totally unaware that he had been followed and that the Tactical Firearms Team had pulled onto the verge a few hundred yards behind him.

Suddenly a black shape leaped through the open car window with a loud yowl. Claws stuck into him, and he thought he saw the gleam of bright yellow eyes. The force and suddenness of the creature's leap onto him forced the gun downwards towards his private quarters and his finger to connect with the trigger not once but twice. The black shape was gone in an instant and he screamed and screamed in pain. The yells were positively unearthly.

It was in fact the Tactical Firearms Team who saved his life. They had been close enough that they charged fully armed to the scene when they heard the shots, and they immediately disarmed Kenny and summoned an ambulance. One of the team did what he could to staunch the flow of blood as another communicated with the ambulance service.

"Gentleman seems to have shot himself," he said. "Doesn't seem to have learned to keep the safety catch on."

Kenny screamed, "It was a wild beast, a panther that did it."

The head of the team shook his head ignoring Kenny's screams.

"No such wild beasts around here but perhaps shooting yourself is just the lesson you needed."

A paramedic was quickly on the scene followed by the Air Ambulance carrying a doctor. The police and emergency services dealt with the complicated situation of facilitating an arrest and saving the suspect's life. Meanwhile a police unit was in control of Kenny's warehouse elsewhere.

As the Air Ambulance went on its way with the doctor muttering something about life changing injuries, and the Tactical Firearms Team packed up and departed, a forensics team arrived to examine the car. Soon there was just a couple of forensics officers and unarmed constables at the scene. In the light set up for the forensic team, one of the police constables spotted a black cat with yellow eyes sitting on top of a nearby drystone wall.

"What are you doing there, pussycat?" he asked.

"Miaow," said Mr Perkins as he jumped down and rubbed himself around the police officer's legs.

"You take care to keep out of the road," said the officer in a kindly way.

Mr Perkins climbed onto the footpath, his tail erect, and walked into the darkness away from the direction of the village.

If any of the villagers heard the gunshots, they assumed the bangs had something to do with the fireworks. Most of them were too absorbed with the celebrations or clearing up to take much notice of the helicopter. As Sabrina made her way to the pub at about quarter to one, she was vaguely aware of the sound of a helicopter.

"Hope no one has had a nasty smash," she commented to Reg.

"Hope not," he said.

The customers had all left the pub and the staff had gone. Glancing around at the empties Sabrina asked,

"What can I do to help?"

"I didn't ask you here to clear up," responded Reg gently, "I asked you here because I have something very specific to ask you… and if you say 'No' I will entirely understand."

Sabrina sat on a bar stool. She suspected what he might ask.

Reg took the ring out of his pocket. The words just seemed to dry up, but he went down on one knee and held the ring out to her, his eyes pleading with her.

"Yes," said Sabrina, "a hundred times yes."

After that Sabrina and Reg just sat together quietly for a very long time with Brandy purring beside them. Nothing else needed to be said.

Just a few miles away near the fingerpost signpost pointing to the village, the old oak tree was now bare of leaves making it easy for a cat to scramble up the tree's naked branches. Mr Perkins sat on a branch near the top of the tree. One could just see a few lights from the village twinkling in the distance from this height. The fireworks were well and truly over, and the majority of people would be fast asleep. Soon it would be dawn and gradually it would get light, and people would be waking up to a new day, a new year and new beginnings.

Could Mr Perkins foretell that Lenny would grow in confidence and particularly enjoy her last year at primary school? Maybe. Could he foretell that Lennie and Nathan would not be fazed by going to the local high school later in the year and that Nathan had made serious steps to train Smokey to be a therapy cat? Perhaps. Could he foresee that Miss Deamer and Miss Dymock would be content with their dogs or that Aunt Lavinia would be similarly contented with Bella and Carmen? Could he foretell that the general would be less lonely or that Sabrina and Reg would have a quiet but joyous spring wedding? Could he foresee that the village would soon have green leaves and spring flowers and new life?

Mr Perkins looked quietly satisfied. His work here was done. He climbed down from the tree and sauntered off into the undergrowth, tail pointing straight upwards, perhaps to look for mice or voles. After all, he was just a cat.

A Cat's Lesson

Information from Mr Perkins

Assistance and Support Animals

The Equality Act 2010 section 173 defines assistance animals (dogs) to whom legal discrimination laws apply. Under the Equality Act 2010, users of assistance dogs have a right not to be discriminated against based on their disability. There is no such legal protection relating to emotional support animals. Assistance dogs are defined as dogs trained to guide a blind person, dogs trained to guide a deaf person, dogs trained by certain charities to assist someone with a disability and dogs trained to assist people with certain prescribed disabilities.

'Guide dogs' https://www.guidedogs.org.uk/about-us/ is a well-known charity which devotes its resources to providing guide dogs for blind people. It says -

'We're a charity, almost entirely funded by donations, and we are the world's largest assistance dog organisation. As world leaders in puppy socialisation and dog training, we're the only organisation to breed and train guide dogs in the UK.'

'Hearing dogs for deaf people' https://www.hearingdogs.org.uk/about/ train intelligent dogs to aid deaf people, from hearing a smoke alarm to hearing a baby's cry. Sometimes their jobs will be to reconnect with aspects of life and combat loneliness.

Assistance dogs uk https://www.assistancedogs.org.uk/ describes its functions:

'**Assistance dogs are highly trained to support disabled people and people with medical conditions in a variety of ways.**

Assistance Dogs UK is a coalition of assistance dog organisations that have been accredited by Assistance Dogs International (ADI) and/or The International Guide Dog Federation (IGDF). ADUK members are non-profit organisations that work to the highest standards of assistance dog training and welfare. From guide dogs to medical alert dogs, from autism dogs to hearing dogs, our members train assistance dogs that change, and often save, the lives of their owners.'

While there is not the legal protection for having an emotional support animal there are one or two charities who do support people in having emotional support animals since many would argue these animals improve quality of life and aid mental health.

Thus far therapy cats in England and Wales are rare. In North America they are more common, for example Baxter a well-known therapy cat has his own Facebook page and many followers.

Pet Rescue

As for the support of animals there are many organisations in the UK which support different aspects of the welfare of pets from the RSPCA to the PDSA and the Blue Cross.

The RSPCA is the main organisation involved in enforcement of animal welfare laws. https://www.rspca.org.uk/.

Also pre-eminent in the protection of cats in the UK is Cats Protection. https://www.cats.org.uk/about-cp. They say,

'We help an average of 157,000 cats and kittens every year thanks in no small part to our network of over 210 volunteer-run branches and 34 centres.'

It should not be forgotten that there are many smaller organisations which help cats and kittens. Fortunately, there are people who love cats and kittens in most parts of cities and villages. For example, in a village in North Lincolnshire is Burton on Stather Cat Rescue. Organisations such as this are listed on a website known as Cat Chat. www.catchat.org/shelter_centre

In the USA media personality Jackson Galaxy has done much to publicise cat rescue https://bestfriends.org/partners/jackson-galaxy-foundation and there are many different organisations and countless websites.

Cat and dog rescue is a much needed international phenomenon with rescue organisations in all types of places, even small islands, for example Cats in Need Menorca. catsinneedmenorca.org.

In the UK, the Dog's Trust is the largest charity rehoming and rescuing dogs. https://www.dogstrust.org.uk/.

There are of course many other dog rescue charities in the UK, a good example being Jerry Green Dog Rescue. https://www.jerrygreendogs.org.uk.

This charity operates in Lincolnshire, Nottinghamshire and South Yorkshire and has been operating since 1961.

British Sign Language and the Deaf Community

British Sign Language is said to be the fourth indigenous language of the British Isles after English, Welsh and Scots Gaelic. It is used by about 90,000 deaf people as their preferred first language. Much information can be gleaned from the National Deaf Children's Society. www.ndcs.org.uk/ .

Solicitors and Charities

Two of the characters were practicing solicitors. Their conduct is governed by the Solicitors' Regulation Authority.

https://www.sra.org.uk/.

It is not unusual for solicitors to become involved with local charities which are of course regulated by the Charity Commission. https://www.gov.uk/government/organisations/charity-commission.

Acknowledgements

And a message from Mr Perkins

I would like to thank Burton on Stather Cat Rescue for letting my husband and I adopt our two tortoiseshell cats. I would like to thank our black cat Tom for being the model and/or inspiration for the drawings of Mr Perkins. He was originally rescued with his brother Charlie by Cats' Protection.

This book is intended to be a work of fiction. No-one says you have to get a dog or a cat if it doesn't suit you. No-one says all dogs and cats are well behaved either. Sadly, some dogs are not suitable to be family pets, and some people have allergies to some pet fur. You don't have to get a dog or a cat or indeed acquire any information or insight from Mr Perkins' adventures. But if you do meet Mr Perkins, he probably does have something important to say to you even if it is only 'Miaow'. He may give you a few purrs if you give him some cat treats. He is after all, just a stray black cat with yellow eyes; isn't he?

Information about Suzanne Stephenson

And her books

I would like to thank you for taking the time to read my books. If you have a moment to spare to review the book you have been reading, I would appreciate it. You may have your own thoughts about what I have written and that is fine. I was a lawyer for many years and then a District Judge. Any legal background is inspired by my long legal career although I hasten to stress the fictional nature of the humans. I am also privileged to live in the English countryside, surrounded by animals who provide a lot of inspiration, as did the bear I saw on holiday in Canada who sparked off the ideas for 'Bearswood End'. I enjoy sketching and the animal pictures are often sketches of animals around the farm. I sometimes think the animals are in charge.

I want to give particular thanks to Sarah Luddington from Mirador Publishing who took me and the animal inspired books under her wing.

If you want to contact me, please feel free to look at my Instagram page:

Suzanne Stephenson (@bearswood_end).

Or contact me through the website:

https://stephensons-authors.co.uk/

Email address: adventures@stephensons-authors.co.uk

The following are books I have written:

Bearswood End

A scientist wanders out into the wilderness and finds a mysterious village populated by bears. To be accurate the bears find him. Can the secret village of the bears survive a threat from the outside world? Read the scientist's diary and the story of the woman who finds it.

Mr Perkins takes Charge

A black cat walks into a solicitors' office. Lives change of the lawyers and people who cross this cat's path, usually for the better. Is he just a stray cat and is it all a co-incidence or is there something more mysterious afoot? If you like cats, you may find this intriguing. If you are just curious about the goings-on of a lawyers' office satisfy your curiosity following the trail of sunshine left by Mr Perkins' paws.

Forever Waste

This is a legal satire about activities at a combined court in a fictional northern town. Two young people arrive whose lives might otherwise have gone to waste and make fresh starts in this fictional town which boasts as main industries a waste plant and a sausage factory. Meet the judges, MPs and other local characters. You will find romance against the background of the court, its lawyers and judges and this northern city and its politicians, and there is even an election in the city. You will also understand the highs and lows of the local football club, and you may even decide to copy a few recipes.

The World According to Patrick White

This is a comic tale with a pinch of satire about a lawyer who finds she has a talking pig, and we discover how he sees the human world and what he thinks of some of our habits and human foibles. Find out how the lawyer and her family cope with this pig of a situation. Needless to say, pig and human have a few adventures before the tale is over, including a court case where the pig is an expert witness and an encounter with a Royal dignitary.

A Cat's Judgement, Mr Perkins lays down the law

That mysterious black cat shows up at a bed and breakfast and a courthouse and things begin to change. Whether it is pet rescue, support animals or British sign language make your mind up if this is a stray moggy or is there a little bit of stardust on his paws?

The Tale of Philida Thrush, A Children's poem about nature, home and community

When a song thrush has her nest demolished by the builders what can a bird do but look around town for a new home? Assisted by her friends Philida goes on a quest to find somewhere to live.

Santa Pig, The Trials of Patrick White

Meet Patrick White the talking pig again. He finds himself involved with the Parish Council and on trial. Will he be able to save the local Christmas festivities? This is a comedy of pigs, law and Christmas which like seasonal punch, should be enjoyed for warm seasonal cheer, or just enjoyed for a bit of laughter at humans' expense.

www.ingramcontent.com/pod-product-compliance
Lightning Source LLC
Chambersburg PA
CBHW061952070426
42450CB00007BA/1289